ADVANCED LANGUAGE TOOL KIT

Teaching the Structure of the English Language

Paula D. Rome

Jean S. Osman

EDUCATORS PUBLISHING SERVICE

CAMBRIDGE AND TORONTO

ACKNOWLEDGMENTS

The work of Dr. Samuel T. Orton, Mrs. June Lyday Orton, Dr. Paul Dozier, Miss Anna Gillingham and Miss Bessie Stillman, provided the foundation on which the *Advanced Language Tool Kit* is based. We owe much to all of them for their pioneer efforts. We are grateful to Mrs. Margaret B. Rawson, master language therapist and author, for her interest and guidance.

Paula D. Rome
Jean S. Osman

Printed in U.S.A.
ISBN 0-8388–0549-3

10 PAH 21

AUTHORS' NOTE

The *Language Tool Kit* was first published by Educators Publishing Service* in 1972, and now with the publication of the *Advanced Language Tool Kit* a continuum is presented, starting with the requisites for teaching elementary level language and advancing through to the more complex requisites for teaching language at the college level.

The *Advanced Language Tool Kit* provides an overview of the structure, organization, and sound units that are needed to develop skills for advanced reading and spelling. The material presented primarily focuses on syllable patterns and on words combining affixes and roots. In working with students at this level, one needs to be aware that most teacher training programs do not teach language analysis in the way that meets the needs of the older dyslexic student. Many teachers will find, therefore, that they must study the language and think about words in quite a different way. Because it is impossible to learn all of the pertinent information quickly or to find the necessary references in one or two books, those beginning in the field of education should be assured that they need be only a few steps ahead of their students. Sometimes students, too, are reassured that teachers do not know everything and are willing to say, "I'm not sure why that word is spelled/pronounced that way, but I'll find out for us."

Although the *Advanced Language Tool Kit* was written with teaching the language disabled student in mind, it contains material that every student of English should know— how our language is put together, the languages from which it is derived, the Latin and Greek roots, and the rules which govern spelling. Learning about one's language can be a fascinating life time study.

It is strongly suggested that those who use this material read it through in its entirety to obtain an overview of the contents and organization. This will also provide a better understanding of the student's problem, the first, most important step, and the teaching rationale presented.

*Future references to Educators Publishing Service will be noted as EPS.

Table of Contents

1. INTRODUCTION

Specific Language Disability—Dyslexia

Dyslexia, an often misunderstood term, derives from the Greek roots *dys* meaning "difficulty" and *lex* meaning "word." Many terms have been used in referring to this disability. Doctors Hinshelwood and Morgan, English ophthalmologists, were the first to publish articles describing the problem (in 1895 and 1896); they called it both "Dyslexia" and "Congenital Word Blindness." Other terms used in identifying this problem include Specific Language Disability, Language Learning Disability, Developmental Reading Disorder, Visual and/or Auditory-Perceptual Handicaps, Strephosymbolia, Mirror Reading, Minimal Brain Dysfunction, Special Learning Disability, and Perceptual-Motor Handicap. Sometimes it has inaccurately been referred to as Minimal Brain Damage. There has never been any conclusive research which documents a relationship between Developmental Dyslexia and brain damage. Research conducted in this field indicates a neurophysiological basis underlying the differences in ability which are causative in dyslexia.

We have chosen to use the generally accepted terms, Specific Language Disability and Dyslexia, interchangeably. The Research Group on Developmental Dyslexia from the World Federation of Neurology, composed of experts in the fields of Neurology, Psychology, Pediatrics, and Education, recommended these two definitions in 1968, and they are still accepted today:

Specific Developmental Dyslexia is "a disorder manifested by difficulty in learning to read despite conventional instruction, adequate intelligence, and socio-cultural opportunities. It is dependent upon fundamental cognitive disabilities which are frequently of constitutional origin."

Dyslexia is "a disorder in children who, despite conventional classroom experience, fail to attain the language skills of reading, writing, and spelling commensurate with their intellectual abilities."

The International Dyslexia Association Research Committee, in collaboration with leaders from the National Center for Learning Disabilities, with scientists from the National Institute of Child Health and Human Development, and with scientists and clinicians from universities in the United States and Canada, adopted the following definition in 1994:

"Dyslexia is one of several distinct learning disabilities. It is a specific language-based disorder of constitutional origin characterized by difficulties in single word decoding, usually reflecting insufficient phonological processing abilities. These difficulties in single word decoding are often unexpected in relation to age and other cognitive and academic abilities; they are not the result of generalized developmental disability or sensory impairment. Dyslexia is manifested by variable difficulty with several forms of language, often including, in addition to problems reading, a conspicuous problem acquiring proficiency in writing and spelling."

Most national and international authorities in the field of Specific Language Disability agree that about 10% of the population has some degree of this disability. Estimates are as high as 15% when those individuals with lesser degrees of the difficulty are included. Dr. Manuel R. Gomez, from the Department of Pediatric Neurology at the Mayo Clinic, in Rochester, Minnesota, stated, "There are more dyslexic students needing recognition and special teaching techniques than all the blind, deaf, and retarded put together." Until recently, most of the research in this area has been undertaken by the medical profession. This research has shown that dyslexia is often familial. For many years authorities thought the problem occurred more frequently in males. Recent research is indicating that the ratio of males to females with dyslexia is much closer.

The primary symptoms of dyslexia are difficulty with reading and spelling, ranging in degrees of difficulty from slow and inaccurate reading and minor inaccuracies in spelling to almost total inability to read and spell. In the early grades, persistent letter reversals and inversions are evident. The letters most often confused or reversed are those that are similar in form, such as b-d, p-q-g, M-W, m-n, u-n, r-n, and f-j-t. Numbers such as 6-9 and 2-5 may also be confused. In the most severe cases, single letter reversals may persist through all of the school years. In the less severe cases, reversals and confusions of letters usually do not persist much beyond second grade, but the sequence of letters within words may be confused and letters may be omitted or added. The student with dyslexia may misread or misspell words such as 'big' for dig or pig, 'from' for form, 'begin' for benign, 'defying' for dignifying, 'preserve' for persevere, or write 'afriad' for afraid, 'invatation' for invitation, 'vister' for visitor, etc. Since short spelling lists can be memorized for a brief time, the student can receive a fairly good grade on a spelling test which has been announced ahead of time. However, review tests, compositions, and informal letters and notes reveal the individual's spelling disability. Younger children of average or higher intelligence are sometimes able to memorize the limited reading vocabulary offered in the early grades, and their language processing problems may not become clearly evident until later grades.

Those children with milder problems may be able to "survive" until junior high school. They will be able to read well enough to "get by," though their reading is slower and more difficult, and they exhibit many errors. Their spelling is usually very poor. Unless the problem is identified, the errors are often attributed to carelessness, lack of motivation, poor handwriting, etc. Bright students with very mild problems may often complete high school successfully. If they continue on to college, they then are apt to experience problems because of the increased demands for reading and writing and a requirement to study a foreign language.

By the time a student is in junior high school, the ability to achieve in academic subjects is almost completely dependent upon the adequacy of language skills. The dyslexic student may then begin to "underachieve" or fail. The cumulative effect of years of frustration, stress, and pressure may take its toll. This can result in behavioral symptoms ranging from personality changes such as withdrawal or "acting out" to truancy and delinquency. Often the student complains of physical symptoms, headaches, eye strain, stomach upsets, etc. All of these symptoms can appear in the younger disabled student whose problem has gone unrecognized.

Dyslexic students who successfully complete high school usually have several positive factors in their favor to help them survive emotionally as well as academically, such as an exceptional ability in sports, music, art, mathematics, social skills, and/or mechanics. Success in non-academic areas helps students feel good about themselves and win the respect of their peers. Families with members who understand and accept poor school achievement without fostering a sense of failure, and supportive teachers, who focus on the positive aspects of a student's school work, help dyslexic students complete their schooling. Extra help with school work from family members and teachers, as well as special classes at school, will typically be a part of the school experience of the language disabled students who complete high school. Unfortunately, there are other students who never achieve academic success—they stay in school and are passed along from grade to grade. They join the nation's ranks of illiterate, unskilled, underemployed or unemployed adults. Fortunately, the problem is receiving increased publicity through the media, and more individuals with dyslexia are beginning to seek help.

Students with dyslexia never have difficulty with reading (decoding) without an accompanying difficulty with spelling (encoding). Often in the less severe cases, the child may have "adequate" reading skills but will have significant difficulty with spelling. Reading and spelling are dependent upon the same language function: the ability to picture or visualize words accurately in the "mind's eye." Reading is the simpler language process; it involves only the recognition of a series of symbols which are already printed. Spelling is the more complex written language process; it demands the recall and writing of a series of symbols without the aid of visual cues.

For the older student, writing compositions is the most difficult challenge. It requires not only the ability to spell accurately, but the knowledge of the rules relating to grammar, punctuation, and syntax. It also requires the ability to organize verbal concepts. These skills usually present serious problems for a student with dyslexia.

In order to understand the learning process, one must think in terms of the three intake pathways—visual (seeing), auditory (hearing), and kinesthetic-tactile (the sensations provided by the feeling of muscle movement). A blind person learns through the sense of hearing and the senses of movement and feeling. A deaf person learns through seeing and movement and feeling; to master speech, awareness of the sensations of the speech musculature is essential. A person who is both blind and deaf still has the muscle movement-feel pathway with which to learn. One has only to think of Helen Keller to realize that people so afflicted can be taught, but it takes a very special method of teaching to reach people so disabled. Obviously, the dyslexic individual is not as handicapped as the blind and/or deaf student, but he/she, too, requires special teaching techniques.

Though the three pathways do not function separately, it is useful to think about them separately in terms of the ways they affect learning. Statisticians and other professionals find the bell-shaped curve a convenient means of expressing the distribution of human abilities in a population. When talking about dyslexia, using this normal curve illustrates that there is a range of problems instead of an all-or- nothing situation. Reading ability, like other skills, exists in degrees from superior to average, poor, or non-existent. A review of the research in this area shows that it can be reasonably assumed that the "normal curve" of population distribution will apply to the range of abilities and disabilities under consideration.

The visual pathway is the most important pathway involved with the acquisition of written language skills. Visual processing ability or visual imagery for words does not refer to actual seeing but to what happens to the visual images in the brain after the eye has received them. A normal curve for visual processing ability would look like this:

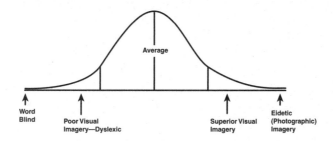

The distribution of visual processing ability or visual imagery for word patterns ranges from exceptional to non-existent. Some people have what is called a "photographic memory," scientifically termed "eidetic imagery." They are able to look at a page of print and "photograph" it in their "mind's eye." Though the image does not usually remain permanently, it does last for a period of time. Obviously, for these people and for all those at the upper end of the distribution curve who have good visual imagery, the recognition and recall of words is extremely simple. It seems that no one need teach this group of students to read, for they are able to do so almost automatically; they often start to read simple words and sentences by kindergarten—from exposure to television, words on boxes, road signs, etc. They never need formal teaching of phonics or spelling rules.

Individuals who have average visual imagery for words will learn by any conventional system of teaching. Some, of course, will need more repetition and practice with skills than others.

At the lower end of the curve are those individuals with poor visual imagery. They range from the very few who are completely "word blind" to those who have relatively minor problems with reading and a more marked degree of difficulty with spelling and composition. This 10% to 15% comprise the total group which can be described as being dyslexic. within this group there are those who range from having difficulty to those who have a disability. The cut-off point is presently determined by the diagnostician's awareness of the problem, the tests used for measurement, and the criteria used for definitions. This fact, in our opinion, leads to much of the misunderstanding of the use of the term dyslexia and the reports of variation of incidence of the disability found in different studies.

Visual imagery for words is not directly related to intelligence. One can be very intelligent and yet have great difficulty learning to read and write well. Thomas Edison, Hans Christian Anderson, Albert Einstein, President Woodrow Wilson, General George Patton, Winston Churchill, Bruce Jenner (Olympic Decathlon winner), Tom Cruise, and many others are witness to this possibility. Conversely, there are many people with below average potential who have no difficulty mastering the mechanics of reading and spelling, even though their intellectual capabilities and educational futures are limited.

This same normal curve of distribution can be applied to the auditory pathway of learning.

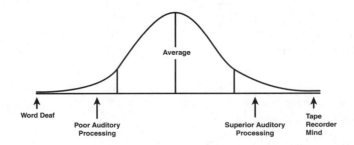

Auditory processing ability does not refer to actual hearing (acuity) but, rather, to what happens to sound impulses in the brain after the ears have received them. This can be illustrated in two separate areas. First, it can be thought of in terms of one's "ear" for music. Some people have perfect or absolute pitch, and would fall at the extreme right of the curve, while those who would fall within the next portion of the scale have an excellent "musical ear." The largest portion of the population has average musical memory for recognizing and recalling tunes. Then there are those who have a "poor ear" or memory for music; no matter how often they hear a song, they have great difficulty remembering the tune or knowing whether or not they are singing on key. At the extreme left of the curve are those people who are tone deaf. It is important to understand that no direct relationship exists between one's "musical ear" or memory and one's intelligence. There can be geniuses who are tone deaf or individuals with average or below average intelligence who have perfect pitch.

Auditory facility with musical tones is not related to facility with words. These attributes are separate and distinct. The example of the musical "ear" is referred to because it often helps clarify thinking about the "verbal ear" or one's "ear" for words. There are people who have what could be considered a "tape recorder" or "phonographic mind" for verbal material. They are able to attend a lecture and come away quoting the speaker almost word for word. They might not have understood all of what was presented, but they seem to be able to "replay their tape," so to speak, and to rehear all of the speaker's words in their "mind's ear." These people have excellent auditory processing abilities (auditory memory, retention, sequencing, and perception). For them, the verbal skills associated with words and ideas, memorizing, remembering what has been said or read, and learning to speak foreign languages are extremely easy, except for the limitations which can result from lack of basic intellectual capacity.

Most individuals have auditory processing abilities which allow them to function adequately. However, for some, any task involving auditory processing of language presents problems. Their mental "tape recorders" do not work efficiently and can cause significant difficulties. For these individuals, spoken language may develop at a later age, enunciation may be poor, and mispronunciations may be common. They have trouble memorizing such things as history dates, the multiplication tables, algebraic theorems, word definitions, or the lines for a play. They often have trouble comprehending material, even when concepts are at their level of understanding and they are able to decode the words. They also may have difficulty in following oral directions, particularly if the directions are spoken too quickly or if too many are given at one time. They may experience difficulty if directions are spoken in an area where there are other distracting sounds, particularly language sounds. As with visual imagery, one's auditory processing ability is not directly related to intelligence. An individual with trouble in this area, however, may never be able to function verbally on a level commensurate with his/her functioning in other areas. Sometimes, when the auditory processing problem is severe, the individual may appear far less intelligent than he/she actually is, and will need long term and specialized teaching in order to learn how to compensate adequately. Research indicates that approximately 60% of those with visual processing problems also have auditory processing problems.

Finally, one can consider the normal distribution curve in terms of the third pathway of learning, the kinesthetic-tactile.

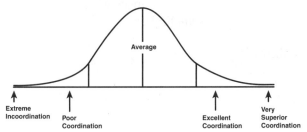

A certain percentage of the population is born with excellent gross motor coordination. These are the children who learn at an early age to walk, feed themselves, tie their shoelaces, ride a two-wheeler, etc. They are usually the "natural-born athletes." Most individuals are born with average coordination skills which develop at an average rate. Some individuals, however, are born with poor coordination and have difficulty mastering simple physical tasks. If severe enough, their condition is medically termed dyspraxia; in lay terms this means "clumsy."

No direct relationship exists between one's physical coordination and one's intelligence. There are people with superior athletic ability who do not have superior intellectual capacities and, conversely, there are those with poor coordination and excellent intellectual abilities.

For the poorly coordinated individuals whose fine motor movements are a problem, dysgraphia (poor handwriting) can make it difficult to produce legible script or to sustain writing tasks for a period of time. The inability to form letters adequately should not be confused with the typical spelling errors made by the dyslexic student, although the dyslexic student may have this added problem. Those with dysgraphia need particular training techniques to develop skills in letter formation. The older student with dysgraphia should be taught keyboarding and encouraged to practice until the skill becomes mastered.

In judging the intellectual capacity of students with dyslexia, one must be aware that the scores obtained on tests are not dependable. Tests rely mainly on symbol recognition and/or reading ability, thus automatically penalizing the student with dyslexia because of the very nature of his/her problem. A student's performance on tests may cause teachers to lower expectations, mislabel a student as having lower potential, and may deprive a student of appropriate help. A language disability is often overlooked as the primary cause for poor academic performance. A student of superior ability may have average grades and thus may not be encouraged and helped to perform at a level commensurate with his or her potential. When there is a question of potential, an individual IQ test should be administered by a qualified educational or clinical psychologist with special knowledge and awareness of dyslexia. The Wechsler Intelligence Scale for Children-III (WISC-III) and the Wechsler Intelligence Scale for Adults-Revised (WAIS-R), used for students over the age of sixteen, are particularly good, since two scores are obtained—one measuring performance tasks involving non-verbal material and the other measuring verbal tasks. It would be preferable if "numbers" and IQ scores were not used to consider placing or to place individuals in programs for special help. But, as long as inaccurate judgments are made, individual testing is indicated whenever there is doubt.

Unless the dyslexic student is provided with the necessary special teaching techniques, reading (decoding) and spelling (encoding) will lag far behind grade level or the level of achievement expected as compared to intellectual capacity. The student's educational future will be jeopardized.

The *Language Tool Kit* is concerned with more elementary material. It is designed to help a teacher, parent, or tutor teach the basic written language skills to students with Specific Language Disability. It can be easily adapted to work with groups of students and is designed for teaching elementary vocabulary. It can also be used for secondary students and adults whose reading skills are still at an elementary level. It provides the instructor with the necessary knowledge of phonics, the rules and patterns governing spelling, a description of drillwork procedures and lesson planning, possible ways of spelling the various sounds of our language, and a list of common non-phonetic words which the student needs to memorize.

The *Advanced Language Tool Kit* is designed to be used with junior and senior high school, college students, and with adults with written language disabilities. If the individual's disability is severe, the material in the *Language Tool Kit* should be mastered first or should be used along with the material in the *Advanced Language Tool Kit*. As has been noted, the two sets of materials present a continuum, starting with the elements required for simpler language and advancing through the most complex. Most older students need the stimulation of working with advanced language materials and structure, even though this material often needs to be presented to them in a simplified form. Some elementary students who are academically gifted and verbally oriented are ready for and will benefit from the material in the *Advanced Language Tool Kit*.

The individual with a language disability must be provided with a specific teaching approach which coordinates the simultaneous use of all three pathways of learning. Those individuals with insecure visual memory for word patterns need the extra reinforcement provided by auditory and kinesthetic teaching techniques. Those students with both visual and auditory perceptual problems will need instruction that places tremendous emphasis on kinesthetic reinforcement techniques. Detailed descriptions of these techniques are presented in the Drillwork Procedures section of the *Language Tool Kit* and the *Advanced Language Tool Kit*.

These teaching principles utilizing a three-pathway approach were formulated in the 1920s by Dr. Samuel T. Orton, then director of the Iowa State Psychopathic Hospital and Professor of Psychiatry at the University of Iowa. Orton was a pioneer in recognizing and studying dyslexia in both its neurophysiological and its educational aspects. Specializing in language disorders, he continued his work during the nineteen-thirties and forties in New York City. Dr. Orton was Professor of Neurology and Neuropathology at Columbia University and Neuropathologist at the New York Neurological Institute from 1932 to 1936. During this period he directed a language research project at the Columbia-Presbyterian Medical Center with funds from the Rockefeller Foundation. His research associate and clinical director was Dr. Paul Dozier. Under Dr. Orton's guidance, Dr. Dozier subsequently headed the Language Rehabilitation Clinic at the Institute of the Pennsylvania Hospital in Philadelphia (1937-1942). It was there that Paula Dozier Rome, the senior author of this publication, received her training from Dr. Dozier.

Anna Gillingham, a psychologist, remedial teacher, and an associate of Dr. Orton's, worked with a group studying language disabilities. She was asked to assume the task of analyzing the structure of the English language and combining this with the teaching procedures recommended by Dr. Orton. That study led to the beginning of her work on a teaching manual. Working together in Honolulu in 1936, Bessie W. Stillman and Anna Gillingham wrote the first edition of the Gillingham Manual, *Remedial Training for Children with Specific Disability in Reading, Spelling and Penmanship*. In the years that followed, several revised and expanded editions were published, and Anna Gillingham trained many teachers in schools and clinics throughout the country.

Others following Dr. Orton's teaching principles have developed additional guidelines and materials. Experience with many different students and groups has led to some adaptations and modifications. This is acceptable within the framework of the Orton-Gillingham approach and adds to its flexibility. It was Dr. Orton who warned against over-standardization, ". . . lest the procedures become too inflexible and be looked upon as a routine method applicable to all cases of non-readers."*

In establishing goals and measuring progress while working with students with dyslexia, one must be aware that there is variation from student to student and from group to group. For students with limited mental ability, the goal is the development of reading and spelling skills which will enable them to survive in a literate society—skills such as reading necessary labels, directions, manuals, signs, forms, driver's license test questions, and writing decipherable messages for family members or employers, etc. For students of superior mental ability, the goal is to develop skills that will enable them to complete their higher education, through graduate school if indicated, though it might require an extra year or more to complete their work. Students of any age with a severe problem will have to learn to cope with a slower reading rate and perhaps to make use of tape recorded reading assignments and compositions, as well as using other compensatory measures.

*Samuel T. Orton, *Reading, Writing and Speech Problems in Children* (Austin, Texas: Pro. Ed., Inc., 1989), 131: (New York: W. W. Norton & Co., 1937), 131. Available from the International Dyslexia Association, Baltimore, Maryland 21286.

Most students become frustrated and disheartened by failures in school. Occasionally a student will become so upset that she/he can no longer function in a classroom situation and might require counseling to help resolve the emotional problems which have developed. When this help has been provided, a program of educational remediation is more readily accepted. Usually an explanation of the language disability and repeated assurances that such a disability does not mean one is "stupid" helps the student accept the special work. The student should also be assured that this approach will be successful and that it is different from the previous programs which have not entirely met his/her special needs. Then the language teacher must demonstrate from the beginning of their work together that the student can succeed—a true challenge!

The Orton-Gillingham procedures can be used with students of all ages. Each student must master the recognition of printed symbols and their appropriate sound equivalents. Spelling rules and generalizations must be learned so that the correct responses become automatic. This takes time, much drillwork, repetition, and encouragement, particularly when the disability is severe. The older student, with a less severe problem which has not been identified until later in the school years or even into adulthood will not necessarily need all of the basic steps outlined. Such a student may be able to start with learning syllable patterns and the affixes and roots, but needs to learn them both visually and auditorily, and with kinesthetic reinforcement while he/she progresses through the advanced materials. Review or introduction to some of the more elementary rules and sound units must be included if they have never been taught or were not mastered.

Teaching with this approach requires flexibility. Procedures must be adapted to the needs of each student or group. Many excellent materials employing the Orton-Gillingham method are available through EPS in Cambridge, Massachusetts.

As soon as a parent or teacher notices the typical symptoms of dyslexia in a student of any age, appropriate intervention should be initiated. Sometimes the symptoms of the disability are misinterpreted, and a student is labeled as lazy, immature, a day dreamer, unmotivated, etc. Early intervention will help the student avoid experiencing failure and frustration, and eliminate the development of counterproductive habits that must then be "unlearned," such as guessing or skipping words not recognized.

Since, by conservative estimates, at least one out of ten of the overall population has some difficulty with the acquisition of written language skills, students need to understand that they are part of a large group and are not unique. Studies have shown that dyslexic students constitute a large proportion of those who drop out of school. Antisocial behavior may result when these students cannot successfully cope with the conventional academic situation. Statistics in studies of facilities for the emotionally disturbed, juvenile detention centers, and prisons attest to the price many pay for not having been taught to read and write adequately and often not even well enough to do the most elementary tasks necessary for survival in our literate society.

Careth Ellingson wrote in an article on dyslexia in the *Saturday Review* many years ago, "It would be difficult, if not impossible, to find any other disability affecting so many (an estimated 6 million) children in the United States today, on which so much research has been done, so many thousands of articles written and yet concerning which so very little information has reached the average teacher or physician, to say nothing of parents and the public. These children are as handicapped by the ignorance surrounding their problems as they are by the problem itself." Although this was written thirty years ago, unfortunately, it is still true today. The children grow up to be older students and adults with the problem.

SUGGESTED READING MATERIAL

This introductory explanation is necessarily brief. Anyone working with a student with dyslexia will want to read more about this problem. Listed below are some suggestions for further reading:

1. Thompson, Lloyd, M.D. *Reading Disability: Developmental Dyslexia*, Springfield, Illinois: Charles C. Thomas Co., 1986.

2. Critchley, MacDonald, M.D. *The Dyslexic Child* (2nd Edition). Springfield, Illinois: Charles C. Thomas Co., 1964.

3. Rawson, Margaret. *Dyslexia over the Lifespan: A Fifty-Five Year Longitudinal Study.* Educators Publishing Services, Inc., 1995.

4. Vail, Priscilla L. *About Dyslexia: Unraveling the Myth.* Programs for Education/Modern Learning Press, 1990.

5. Levine, Melvin D., M.D. *Keeping A Head in School.* Educators Publishing Services, Inc., 1990.

6. The *Annals Of Dyslexia*, published by the National Orton Dyslexia Society (now known as the International Dyslexia Association) has many excellent articles pertinent to this level of study. Several we would recommend are:

    a. *Beyond Phonics: Integrated Decoding and Spelling Instruction Based on Word Origin and Structure.* Marcia Henry, *Annals*, 38, 258–275.
    b. *The Structured Flexibility of Orton-Gillingham.* Betty Sheffield, *Annals*, 1991, 41–54.
    c. *Persistent Auditory Dyslexia in Young Dyslexic Adults.* Doris J. Johnson, *Annals*, 1980, 268–276.

Having a standard dictionary which includes information on the origins of words, the affixes and the roots from which they derive is a necessity for the instructor. *The American Heritage Dictionary of the English Language* and *The Random House Dictionary of the English Language* are but two examples of such a resource.

2. ESSENTIAL ELEMENTS FOR A TEACHING PROGRAM

The essential elements for teaching students with a Specific Language Learning Disability* endorsed by members of the International Dyslexia Association include the following. (The Academy of Orton-Gillingham Practitioners and Educators have added the concepts of diagnostic and prescriptive teaching as part of these elements; we have noted them as numbers 9 and 10.)

1. *Multisensory*: A multisensory approach must involve all pathways to learning—auditory, visual, and kinesthetic/tactile. The last involves hand/arm movement, speech musculature movement (lips, tongue, and throat) and the sense of touch.

2. *Alphabetic–Phonetic*: Students need to understand the nature of our form of written language. They need to understand (a) that a letter has both a name and a sound, (b) that a spoken word is made up of a sequence of individual sounds, (c) that letters are sequenced from left to right, and (d) speech sounds match the symbols as they are written.

3. *Synthetic–Analytic*: Decoding (reading) and encoding (spelling) are synthetic and analytic processes. Letters are sounded and blended into words. Syllables are built around vowel patterns and blended into longer words. Spoken words are divided into sequences of sounds, and the symbols representing those sounds are written. Students need to master both synthetic and analytic techniques. Analytic spelling strengthens reading, and conversely, reading strengthens spelling.

4. *Structured:* The English language must be presented in an organized way, involving sounds, rules, syllable patterns, generalizations, grammar, and linguistic principles.

5. *Sequential*: Our language needs to be learned by starting with the simple and moving to the more complex. It needs to be sequenced in an organized way for the study of both the spoken and written language involved in reading and spelling.

6. *Cumulative*: Each new element introduced needs to be directly connected to what is already known, so that it can be readily used as the body of knowledge grows.

7. *Repetitive*: Just understanding the logic of language is not sufficient. Overlearning is necessary so retrieval becomes automatic. This is achieved by repetition. The amount of repetition required is dependent upon the severity of the learning problem.

8. *Cognitive*: Language must be taught in such a way that the logic is apparent and makes sense to the person required to learn it. Understanding why the student is experiencing difficulty learning language, and why it is necessary for the student to learn using this method is an essential part of the process. Reasoning can be used to build mastery.

9. *Diagnostic*: A teacher must be able to observe a student's confusions with letters, sound-symbol associations, sequencing, etc. and understand what elements of the language are required to be taught or reviewed in order to help that student's specific difficulty.

10. *Prescriptive*: A teacher needs to know what teaching steps to prescribe for a student and how to implement those steps into an appropriate instructional plan to assure progress.

---

*The authors acknowledge Betty Sheffield for her contribution to the essential elements for teaching students with Specific Language Learning Disabilities.

3. WORKING WITH OLDER STUDENTS

The term "older student" refers to students from junior high school level on, including adults. The chronological age of individuals is not an accurate measure of their written language skills. For example, one may see an eighth grader who is only a year behind in written language skills, or a high school student or an adult with elementary-level skills. Every variation possible can occur within this skills continuum.

A person's ability to master written or spoken language is determined by several factors:

(a) The individual's intellectual potential.

(b) The type and amount of reading and spelling instruction received.

(c) The person's inherent ability to master language in terms of both the visual and the auditory processing systems.

(d) The language background or the sophistication of spoken language used by the student's family members and friends, and whether or not English is the primary language spoken at home.

There are two general groups teachers of older language disabled students will confront. Group A is made up of students who have had appropriate language training in their earlier school years and, as a consequence, know a fair amount about basic phonics and the rules governing the elementary level of language. Group B is made up of students who have never been identified as having a language processing problem and have had little or no special education. Though they may have been in what their school referred to as special classes, the instruction provided may not have been designed to meet the specific needs of an individual with a language learning disability. These two groups must be taught with the same materials and multisensory teaching techniques. However, the sequence in which the information about language structure, sounds, rules, etc., are introduced will vary.

When teaching a student who has mastered a fair amount of most of the basic tools for dealing with elementary language (Group A), the teacher should start by going through the advanced language information contained in this program. If certain "pieces" of the information are insecure or missing, such as the various ways to spell sounds (multiple spellings), the syllable division rules, etc., the teacher must plan to teach these "pieces."

The teacher can use the Check List of Basic Language Sounds, found on pages 60 and 61, to establish the exact extent of the student's phonic knowledge. (These pages can be photocopied to allow the student to read from the sheets while the teacher keeps track of responses on separate copies.) Another option is, if the teacher owns or has access to the card deck from the *Language Tool Kit*, to use those cards to determine which sounds and rules the student already knows. While checking to see which sounds the student has already learned, the teacher can also ask questions to ascertain which rules are known and which might need review. For example, he/she could ask, "Where do you find <u>ow</u> in a word?," or, "What is the sound for <u>ar</u> at the end of a polysyllabic word?"

The teacher can introduce advanced language concepts and at the same time, teach any of the basic sounds or rules the student does not yet know and review those which are not yet secure. Most teachers are competent readers and spellers and did not have to learn basic phonics, linguistic rules, or the structure of the English language in order to master these skills. Unfortunately, many teachers in their own teacher training programs have not been adequately taught the linguistic concepts required to teach language disabled students. For such teachers, both *Language Tool Kit*s are valuable resources.

Teaching a student who has had no training in language skills or has had a grossly inadequate remediation program (Group B) will present a great challenge. It is recommended that the teacher avoid presenting the stu-

10

dent with single letter consonants and vowels while asking him to read elementary words such as *cat*, *hop*, or *smile*. Though a student may need to learn such language units, the teacher can introduce them while teaching syllable patterns or root words that the student uses and hears in daily conversation and current academic work. For example, the short sound of the letter a can be taught by teaching prefixes such as trans- or ad- and root words such as -act- or -mand-; this makes it possible to read and write words such as *transact* or *demanding*.

Most students will know the sounds for the consonants, so the teacher can start with them by teaching the open syllable pattern. The vowel comes at the end of an open syllable, and its sound is the same as the letter's name. Known consonants can be combined with any one of the five vowels to make open syllables used in longer words. This would allow the student to work with syllables such as pre-, tri- and mo- to spell the first syllable of words such as *pretending*, *triangular* and *modem*. A student may also be taught the sound for -tion and then use it in combination with open syllables, reading and spelling words such as *motion, vacation, recreation, rotation*, etc.

Group B students are reassured when they are told that the reading and spelling in the early stages of their study will consist of single words or phrases with patterns they know or are currently being taught. The teacher can provide lists of words to read that have the long vowel syllable patterns plus the -tion; the same types of words can be dictated for spelling review. In this way, from the first lesson on the student is working with more difficult, adult vocabulary.

When the student can easily read open syllables and spell them from dictation, the teacher can begin to teach the vowel-consonant-e syllable pattern (-ate, -ope, -ine, -use, -eve). This is fairly easy for the student since the vowel in this syllable pattern has its long sound, which is the same as the letter name. The student can soon combine this syllable pattern with the first one learned to read and spell such words as *promote, debate,* and *proscribe.*

After finding out which short vowel sounds the student knows, the teacher can begin to teach the unlearned short vowel sounds, one at a time. The prefixes and root words which have short vowels are an excellent resource for the teacher. Words using these sounds can be given to the student to practice and use when analyzing more difficult or adult vocabulary. For example, knowing the short sound for the letter i would allow the student to work with prefixes such as in-, il-, dis-, dif-, mid-, and mis- and root words such as -dict-, -fin-, and -strict-. This provides the tools to read and spell words such as *invocation, restricting, dictation*, and *finish*.

While working on words with open and closed syllables, along with what the student already knows from the basic pack, the teacher can also begin to introduce the remaining sound units, one or two at a time, using the multisensory techniques discussed in this manual.

The flexibility of this approach allows the student to progress through the sound units at a rate in which he/she can assimilate the information. Learning language using this structured, linguistic, analytical approach will give the student an added advantage; the knowledge of language organized in this way will permit the student to find words in the dictionary more easily.

At some point in discussions about language with an older student, the teacher should mention that 86% of the English language is predictable and regular if one knows all of the sounds, rules, and patterns. Since approximately 14% of words are not phonetic, the student must be made aware that there are a certain number of words which must be memorized. Commonly used words such as *could, through, laugh, buy, beautiful,* and *guarantee* are examples. A list of the most common nonphonetic words in elementary vocabulary can be found in the *Language Tool Kit*. There is a similar list on page 57 of this manual of the *Advanced Language Tool Kit* for higher level vocabulary words. As with younger students, older students should work on two or three of these words at a time. Specific techniques for teaching these words are discussed in the *Language Tool Kit*.

Many teenagers and adults quickly lose interest if they feel the level of instruction is too elementary for them or is too advanced to make sense. The strategy of talking to students about advanced language structure, syllables, affixes, and roots is often the "magic key" to unlock the door. Then, with this group of students, the challenge of planning a program begins. While teaching the six types of syllables, affixes and roots, multiple spelling possibilities for prefixes and suffixes, sentence structure and parts of speech, etc., the teacher will also need to cycle back to teach or reinforce basic rules (when to double consonants before adding suffixes to one syllable words or when to use –ck, –tch, –dge, etc.). The teacher should also introduce the remaining sounds from the basic pack that are still unknown and review those that remain insecure.

The prerequisites for a student to work effectively with the structure of higher level language, which includes polysyllabic words made up of affixes combined with Latin and Greek root words, are:

1. Techniques for sounding and blending together at least five separate speech sounds, which is the minimum number needed by a student attempting to analyze two-syllable words.

2. Knowledge of the six syllable patterns. (See page 27.)

3. Understanding and applying the three primary syllable division rules: (1) V C.C V; (2) V.C V; and (3) V C.V patterns. (See pages 29–31.)

4. The knowledge that higher level language involves the "building" of words from a basic root form; i.e., prefixes are added before the root; suffixes are added after the root. For example, <u>act</u> / re<u>act</u> / <u>act</u>ivate / <u>act</u>ivity / <u>act</u>or / trans<u>act</u> / inter<u>act</u>ing. The concept of extended words is used to describe the category of words with affixes added. In the above example, all but <u>act</u> are extended words. The student then becomes aware that prefixes and suffixes influence the meaning of a root. Suffixes may also determine the part of speech and how the extended word is used syntactically in sentences.

If the student has not yet learned the skills listed, the teacher needs to provide instruction covering these elements before moving on to the material presented in the *Advanced Language Tool Kit*. As noted, a valuable resource for teaching these skills would be the *Language Tool Kit* by Rome and Osman.

The *Advanced Language Tool Kit* provides the teacher with a "bird's eye view" of the structure and organization of words, a necessity for teaching advanced reading and spelling skills. Several good resource books to supplement this information are available. A good dictionary which notes the origins and meaning(s) of roots and affixes of longer words is a necessity. To provide practice for each new "piece of the language" introduced, lists of words using them are needed. They can be found in the resource books listed on page 23 or be created by the teacher. Save every list of words created for practicing a sound, rule, affix, or root pattern, for each can be revised as necessary and used again to meet the needs of future students. From an extensive list of words, the teacher can choose less demanding words for a younger student or one that has a more serious problem and lower level skills. The teacher can also choose more difficult words for the student who is farther along in the study and needs more challenge. Computers have helped to make such a task relatively easy.

One needs to use the skills of a circus juggler! But few things in education are as rewarding as working with these students when their interest has been captured. Enthusiasm, motivation, and confidence build as the language unfolds for them. It is reassuring for them to find that the English language is not a guessing game, and they **can** learn it. The pieces of the "master puzzle" begin to fall into place and, as with picture puzzles, the more pieces in place, the more easily the remaining ones seem to fit in.

4.   MULTISENSORY TEACHING APPROACH

Research indicates that 60% or more of students with some degree of insecure visual memory for words also have some degree of difficulty with auditory memory or processing of spoken language sequences. For these students, kinesthetic training for improving reading and spelling skills is essential and is most often the "missing link" in other reading programs. Most reading programs, even strongly phonetic methods, present words primarily through the visual channel. Carefully sequenced instruction for word attack skills plus intensive auditory and kinesthetic training will provide the student with valuable tools to use while developing oral and written language skills.

Teaching written language skills using a multisensory approach requires that students be taught to use all the intake pathways effectively. They must learn to associate the letter or letter combinations that their eyes are seeing and their ears are hearing with the feel of the correct sound in the speech musculature as the sounds are pronounced. The writing hand must learn to make the association of the feel in the hand and arm as the letter units are formed and as the speech sounds are produced. Students must also be taught to listen carefully to speech sounds, feel them in their own speech musculature, and write the spelling(s) which represent the sounds. Because many students, those recognized as having dyslexia and many not so identified, do not learn this information intuitively or independently, the associations of sounds and symbols using the visual, auditory, and kinesthetic pathways must be directly taught. For some students the kinesthetic pathway of learning is the primary one through which information about the association of speech sounds and written symbols can be learned and retained. Students need to be taught the importance of the feel in their lips, tongue, and throat as sounds are produced, as well as the sequence in which they occur in words. They must also be taught to be attentive to the feel of the movement in the hand and arm while writing sequences of letters, as well as the feel of the speech musculature. Older students may not require large arm muscle movement in order to master writing the sound units. The movements used when writing with pen or pencil may be all that is needed. For example, the feel of the sequence of movement in writing over and over again the endings -<u>ology</u> or -<u>cious</u>, or the root words -<u>struct</u>- or - <u>psycho</u>- while simultaneously sounding aloud, will help the student retain the memory of the sequence of letters. He/she may then be able to recognize that unit when reading or recall it when needed for spelling. With these techniques a student with auditory processing problems can also learn to use word analysis skills to sequence sounds in words which have been difficult to pronounce ('aksed' for asked, 'ambiance' for ambulance, or 'pasgetti' for spaghetti).

When spelling, most people try to visualize the letter patterns when a word is difficult; for someone with dyslexia, that visual recall is not reliable, correct, or retrievable. To compensate, the arm and mouth must "pay close attention to one another." If the student is not sounding words or syllables subvocally or aloud while writing, he/she may miss valuable clues that would help compensate for the insecure visual memory for words. When a student is uncertain of a word or is unable to analyze the sequence of the letters and sounds in a word while reading, the muscle feel resulting from tracing the letters may trigger a correct response. Retrieving the correct sound may not be possible if the student merely continues to look at the word, using only visual clues. The teacher cannot assume that students will easily understand the concept of using multisensory techniques when learning and attacking unfamiliar language units or words. Many students must be taught step-by-step and provided with situations in which to practice each step repeatedly. A teacher working with a student who has had earlier multisensory training needs to continue incorporating the kinesthetic training in all of the teaching steps at the advanced level. Through practice, the student will gradually learn to use kinesthetic reinforcement automatically whenever necessary. Teaching the student to use a multisensory approach for the first time is an added challenge. The student may feel that it is babyish or silly to write word units in isolation and to make "unintelligible sounds" aloud while writing. Some students have been told since first grade not to sound aloud while reading or to write quietly. Teachers may have said to the student that vocalizing disturbs other students or will slow him/her down; they have obviously misunderstood the value of having students utilize the other pathways of learning language. To erase the memory of such admonitions, often repeatedly reinforced over the years, the teacher will need to be patient and consistent in establishing the steps for each procedure (reading, spelling, drill work, blending drills, etc.) and help the student gradually overcome habits which are counterproductive.

For some students, an explanation of what dyslexia is and a discussion of how to use the different pathways for learning are enough to convince them to adopt the essential strategies. For most students, the feelings of being scolded by teachers or teased by peers have made such a strong impression, that it may take many weeks or even months of reteaching, encouragement, and repeated explanations before they can gradually assimilate the multisensory techniques into their way of handling words. When working with others nearby, a student can learn to subvocalize in a manner that is not obvious or distracting to them.

5. DRILLWORK PROCEDURES WITH CARDS

I.   Introduction of Word Units

1. The teacher shows the student the card with a new word unit and pronounces the sound for the unit.

2. The student repeats the sound clearly.

3. The student writes the word unit several times while sounding aloud.

4. The meaning and usage of the word unit is discussed along with the schwa sound, if applicable.

5. The student practices the new word unit by reading words which combine it with other sound units already studied.

6. The student uses the new unit in spelling, combining it with those already known, sounding aloud simultaneously.

7. If the new unit causes unusual difficulty, the teacher and student should establish a key word.

II.   Visual Drills

Students need to be able to recognize groups of letters and remember their correct sound association(s). For example, a student looking at the prefix con- will learn that it has two sound possibilities, (kŏn) in words when the accent is on that syllable (con´text, con´template, con´cept) or (kən) in others when the syllable is not accented(kən.tain´, kən.sume´, kən.ven´ient). The use of the visual drill provides the necessary practice. The teacher faces the student across a desk or table. The cards are held upright so the student can see them clearly. The teacher shows the card and the student responds with the sound that the letter combination represents. The sound, or the most important sound for those that have more than one, should be mastered first until the response becomes automatic. Then other listed sounds can be introduced. After a student has been taught more than one sound for a card, she/he should then be expected to respond with those.

If the student has difficulty with the sound of any letter combination, she/he should not be allowed to guess. The teacher helps by asking the student to write the letter(s) on paper to see if kinesthetic cues will trigger recognition and recall. If this is not successful, the student should say the letter names aloud. If the correct sound is still not recalled, the teacher should then ask the student for the "key word" (if one was used when it was introduced). If she/he still cannot recall the sound, the teacher should give the correct response orally and ask the student to repeat and write the letter(s) on paper a number of times, saying the sound aloud simultaneously. This process, using the visual, auditory, and kinesthetic pathways, provides the complete, coordinated reinforcement of the correct response to the unlearned or confused units.

Though tracing may not work every time, it is an effective tool for helping recognition and recall and should never be overlooked when using a multisensory teaching approach. When a student is having particular difficulty learning a correct response, a key word can be useful. The teacher and student together choose a key word which is the most meaningful to the student. The key word should then be used consistently to help trigger the student's memory until the sound becomes securely learned. Recalling the key word should not become part of the student's routine responses during the visual drill, but used only when the student has difficulty remembering the sound unit. Routine use of key words only lengthens drill time and is usually not necessary, particularly at this level. After working with the cards for some time, the student usually knows with certainty the sound associations for most of the units introduced in the early stages of work. Those cards can be removed from the drillwork pack. They should, however, be included occasionally for an overall review.

III.   Auditory Drills

A student will need auditory drills with new material. It is important for him/her to be able to hear the pronunciation of roots and affixes in isolation and to recall and review all the known ways to write them. For example, the suffix sound -əs may be spelled -ess (for females – *waitress*), -ous (for adjectives – *mountainous*), -us - (for nouns – *bonus*), -ice - (for just a few words – *service*). The teacher must realize how important the auditory drill is in teaching reading skills. A student who can recall letter patterns for writing in isolation is more apt to recognize those same patterns when they are seen in print for reading. The card pack should be held so that the student cannot see the information on the back of the card being presented. It is also important that the student look at the teacher's mouth as each sound is pronounced. For each sound the teacher says, the student responds by saying the sound orally and by writing it. Whenever the student has difficulty giving the correct response, the teacher should repeat the sound, asking the student to repeat it as well. This procedure will provide the student with the opportunity to use his or her own kinesthetic and auditory cues for recall. Guessing should not be allowed. If the student cannot respond correctly, he/she should then be shown the unit on the card and asked to write it several times while saying the sound aloud simultaneously. This, again, provides complete, coordinated, multisensory reinforcement, and if there is difficulty with a particular sound unit, use of a key word would be appropriate. Tracing letters on a table can also be a valuable reinforcement drill. For some students, especially those who confuse the sequence of letters needed to write a unit ("is it -sion or -soin?"), reinforcement is added by saying the names of the letters aloud while simultaneously writing them.

Every time the teacher gives a sound which has multiple spelling possibilities, the student should be asked to give as many of the possibilities as he/she has been taught to that point. This can be done orally (giving letter names), but some of the time the unit should be written to take advantage of visual and kinesthetic reinforcement. For example, if the teacher says the sound unit (ən) and the student has been taught to use -en, -an, and -on for that suffix sound, he/she should be expected to spell or write all three possibilities. It is important for the student to establish the habit of giving the multiple spellings in the order in which they are listed. See pages 42–43.

The auditory drill should be retained for as long as the duration of instruction. When word units, be they affixes or roots, are consistently spelled correctly, they may be dropped from the regular drill and included occasionally for review. When the student has mastered those with multiple spellings, they may also be dropped. All of the word units should be reviewed periodically.

If there is time for only one drill during a lesson, the auditory is the better choice. If kinesthetic reinforcement is added, by having responses written, it is even better yet. The auditory drill provides an essential connection between speech sounds and written units, a crucial reinforcement for the student's mastery of words.

IV.   Kinesthetic Drills

The teacher must be vigilant when training the student to use the kinesthetic pathway. Within the kinesthetic framework the two important channels to be used are (a) hand-arm movements and (b) lip, tongue, and throat movements. Techniques for using these two channels simultaneously, when introducing new material and reinforcing learning, are necessary.

The student must learn to become aware of "the feel" of hand-arm movements involved in forming the letter sequences in word units such as trans-, -ology, -cede, etc. Each time the student uses pencil on paper or chalk on chalkboard, or traces on the desk, table, or another surface, learning is reinforced kinesthetically. Handwriting work is important to insure that the formation of letters is correct, so accurate "feel" is provided. If the writing of any particular letter combination presents a problem, extra practice is needed until the student can accurately sequence the letters and write the unit easily. For young students, tracing on a rough surface or in materials such as rice or sand is valuable. However, it is the **movements** made in tracing which are important for reinforcement rather than the nature of the surface upon which the writing is done. For older students, the process of writing with the pencil on paper usually provides enough kinesthetic reinforcement to achieve secure memory. Tracing on the table top is a good enhancement when there is difficulty. Older students are seldom comfortable with sand or rice tracing because they feel it is childish. We have found it to be unnecessary.

The teacher must emphasize the importance of the student's use of their lips, tongue, and throat movements to produce speech sounds and to sequence these sounds for spelling. The importance of the movements of the speech musculature in training the dyslexic students is so often overlooked in most instructional approaches. In order to utilize the reinforcement of these cues, the student is taught that during the lesson she/he should always sound aloud while writing. The sounds that the mouth is making and the ears are hearing must coincide with the letter forms the hand is making. This provides simultaneous reinforcement through the three pathways of learning. In the classroom and in other situations where the student might be embarrassed or others might be distracted, moving the hand and the lips while sounding subvocally can be substituted. The more severe the language disability, the more dependent the student is upon kinesthetic cues. This is particularly true for the students who have auditory processing problems—difficulty with blending and with sound sequences. Students who have markedly impaired auditory and visual processing skills must be trained to rely heavily on the kinesthetic pathway. Kinesthetic drills are often either missing or not stressed enough in programs of instruction for these particular students. These drills are absolutely essential for the severely impaired, so be sure not to neglect or drop them from the repertoire of teaching tools.

V.   Blending Drills

Learning just the sounds associated with the word units on the cards is not sufficient for reading. For some students, blending is an easy process. For others, blending is very difficult and requires much training and practice. The benefits to the student who learns to blend syllables automatically are well worth the often long-term planning and teaching efforts required of the teacher.

The goal of the blending drill is to teach the student to visually recognize any combination of letters or syllables and to respond orally with the appropriate sound(s). Word lists involving the units studied provide the most efficient way to practice blending skills. When students experience difficulty blending single sound units, the same can be expected with syllables. The training process for both involves providing practice in blending two syllables, then three, and so forth. Lists may be made up or found in materials available from EPS or other sources. If the student is a persistent guesser, nonsense words included in a list will help minimize guessing.

The student with auditory processing problems will have more difficulty blending syllables even when she/he can recognize and pronounce them in isolation. In that case, the student needs practice putting syllables together, repeating them aloud to help retain the memory of the "feel" of the correct pronunciation in the speech mechanism and the "sound" of the pronunciation until she/he is secure enough to determine and add the next syllable. The student should then verbalize these two combined syllables at least two or three times for reinforcement. When the blended pronunciation is secure enough, the student can then determine the pronunciation for the third syllable and add it to the first two, etc., until the word is completed. Taking the word 'satisfactory' as an example, the steps would be to blend the syllables as follows: sat + is = satis; satis + fac = satisfac; satisfac + tor = satisfactor; satisfactor + y = satisfactory. Or, in the word 'inconsequential, 'in + con = incon; incon + se

= inconse; inconse + quen = inconsequen; inconsequen + tial = inconsequential. Some students may be able to blend syllables more easily, therefore these detailed blending steps need not be emphasized. The blending of sounds and syllables is crucial to attaining successful decoding skills. The teacher should not be discouraged if much drillwork is needed before the severely impaired student can blend and retain sound sequences accurately. Persistence in this drill work will provide an essential tool in dealing efficiently with polysyllabic words. Starting from the first day, some type of blending work should be part of every lesson.

When teaching comprehension skills, the teacher should continue to keep the same formula in mind, because sequencing information involves the same steps, except that ideas are being blended together rather than sounds or syllables.

VI.   Introducing New Material

When the student seems reasonably secure with the word units studied, the teacher can introduce a new one using the guidelines provided under "Suggested Order of Presentation" for prefixes, roots, or suffixes. Rather than adding a new unit, the teacher may want to introduce the second sound on a card which had already been presented. For example, -ate as ət (climate) after the student has learned the -ate saying (āt) (regulate). Obviously, the speed with which a student is able to learn new units varies greatly according to the degree of disability. For this reason, no specific guidelines or day-to-day lesson plans have been provided in this manual. Each instructor must decide the rate at which new material can be added.

VII.   General Guidelines Concerning Drillwork with Cards

Pencils without erasers, pens, or fine pointed felt pens are recommended for all written work. In this way, the student does not waste lesson time erasing, and the teacher has an indelible record of the particular errors a student makes. By remembering that the student is being taught to use a three pathway approach, the teacher can adjust the drills and the materials used to emphasize the ones necessary to meet the needs of a particular student or small group. If a student is not learning as well as a teacher would expect, his/her techniques of instruction should be reviewed. The teacher can ask, "Am I using enough auditory training for the student?" (That drill is more demanding for the student and the teacher, so it becomes the drill that might be left out of the lesson plan most often.) "Am I including enough kinesthetic reinforcement and teaching the student to use it constantly for learning? Am I providing enough repetition and drillwork for confused word units and newly introduced material?" Accuracy, not speed, should be stressed. A student can learn to read and spell through patient, careful drillwork. The teacher will need to work toward establishment of immediate, automatic knowledge of symbol-sound associations. Reading speed will usually increase gradually as the mechanics of decoding are mastered.

Games and busywork detract from the structured learning process and waste the student's and teacher's time. Occasionally, for the poorly motivated student, the use of games is acceptable, but they should be dropped as soon as this tactic is no longer needed. The success factor which is built into this approach is usually sufficient to provide the necessary motivation.

It is most effective to introduce the student to the easier or more common prefixes, suffixes, and roots first. This allows the student to read and spell more words sooner. During drillwork, the units introduced from each deck (prefix, suffix or root) should be practiced together. This helps to reinforce the concept of their different functions and positions in words. During the drillwork, the cards the student knows in each deck should be presented in random order, and mixed before each lesson, similar to a shuffling a deck of playing cards.

18

6. SUGGESTIONS FOR WORKING WITH GROUPS

The teacher working with groups will find the following suggestions helpful. Ideally, students grouped for language training should be matched as closely as possible using these four factors as guidelines: (1) grade placement, if applicable, (2) intellectual potential, (3) degree of difficulty with auditory processing, (4) degree of difficulty with visual imagery. The size of groups can vary from two to six or more students, but the smaller the group, the more personalized and effective the instruction. From a practical point of view, ideal groups are not always possible. They may have to be larger, and the students may not be as closely matched as one would wish. But, nevertheless, they will all be learning the necessary information and techniques. Standing before the group to present the cards for drillwork is usually the easiest approach for the teacher. Some have found that a small stand with a rack for holding the cards in a slanted position so the students are able to see the card clearly is useful. Arranging the students' desks in a semicircle is a possibility. Special equipment is not a necessity. A teacher can utilize whatever is available to devise the teaching arrangement that best suits the situation.

During visual and auditory card drills, each student should respond individually to a card rather than the group sounding in unison. The students respond, taking turns around the group, until all of the cards have been reviewed. Asking for group response can sometimes provide an interesting change in routine, but it should be considered as an occasional procedure and not a regular practice. If a student gives an incorrect response, the teacher proceeds exactly as when working with students individually, except that in a group situation all of the students write and sound aloud the corrected response. When spelling, the group follows all of the same steps outlined under Lesson Planning, but they repeat in unison and sound aloud as they write.

It is important that all of the students be trained to watch the teacher's mouth while the spelling words are pronounced. The teacher plans the spelling dictation to cover the "practice" needs of individuals within the group. All of the students write the same words, with the teacher helping those students who have the greatest difficulty. (See Section 8, Procedures for Teaching Spelling, page 24.) Correction of errors should be made before dictation continues. The teacher keeps the spelling papers as a reminder of the sound units and spelling rules which need review in subsequent lessons and as a continuous record of the progress and needs of each student.

7. PROCEDURES FOR TEACHING READING

As mentioned previously, older students who need to improve their reading/decoding skills generally fall into two categories: (1) those who have had a foundation of basic sounds and language structure and need to continue on with advanced material, and (2) those who have no foundation in word analysis skills and need to learn the organization and structure of the English language from step one. The chronological age of a student is not the determinant in deciding where to begin. The level at which the student can read and write and how much is already understood about written language are the crucial determinants. There is often a difference in students' reading ability level compared to their spelling level, so that the instructor will have to plan to work in each area at quite different levels. To summarize briefly, start where the student's skills breaks down. The principles of working with the older student involved in reading more complex vocabulary are essentially the same as those used in working with the younger students, except the focus is on working mainly with syllables, roots, and affixes.

Older students with dyslexia continue to have problems retaining secure visual images of words. When they have difficulty reading words, they must depend upon their knowledge of phonics and language structure. The longer words in advanced vocabulary still follow the alphabetic/phonetic principles of the English language. They are generally more regular in their patterns than the shorter, more frequently used words which usually derive from the Anglo-Saxon. This is an encouraging fact to emphasize with the older student. It is helpful for them to understand the "levels" of language with which they must deal. This understanding provides more information about the possibilities of appropriate choices for letter groups and patterns for spelling. The following diagram, developed by Dr. Marcia Henry, former professor at San Jose State University, California, and former president of the International Dyslexia Association, is very useful for teachers and students.

This pyramid illustrates that words in our language come from many sources, more from the three lower levels, Anglo-Saxon, Latin, and Greek, and fewer from other languages as one proceeds farther up the pyramid. Samples of some contributions from these languages are:

Anglo-Saxon

- short vowel signals: -ck (back, stick);
  -tch (match, stretch); -dge (bridge, ledge);
  -ll (still, small); -ff (cliff, stuff); -ss (class, discussed)
- doubling rule — (hit–hitting, sag–sagged, forgot–forgotten, commit–committee)
- vowel teams — (moon, rain, seem, boat)

Latin
- k̲ is not used in Latin so word units use c̲:

  ac̲– *accept* ; su̲c̲– *succeed* ; –c̲t̲ tract
- common ending –t̲i̲o̲n̲ — *action, protection*
- common ending –i̲b̲l̲e̲ — *possible, sensible*

Greek
- uses p̲h̲ for the (f) sound — *phonetic, philosophy*
- uses c̲h̲ for the (k) sound — *psychology, chaotic*
- uses y̲ for the (ī)and (ĭ) sounds — *cycle, cybernetic, myth, dyslexia*

Spanish and Italian
- words ending in o̲ — *taco, poncho*
- musical terms — *solo, soprano*

French
- words use c̲h̲ for (sh) — *chenille, champagne*
- words using q̲u̲e̲ as (k) — *unique, antique*
- unusual spelling combinations —

  e̲t̲ as (ā) — *ballet, filet*

  silent s̲ — *Illinois, chamois*

Other languages — Norwegian – *ski*, Dutch – *tattoo*, Tongan – *taboo*, etc.

Other important procedures to follow:

1. The student should be required to follow along under the line of print being read by using a pencil or a finger of the hand used for writing. Some older students have been scolded so often for following along as they read that they refuse to do so. It can be pointed out to the student that fast readers and "scan readers" most often track with their finger when progressing down a page. This may counteract the propaganda about its being babyish. Though less helpful for the student, the teacher may have to "back off" and allow the student to use a card under the line of print. The advantage of a pencil poised under the words being read is that the student can, if needed, use the pencil to trace the letters within the word, underline vowel patterns, or mark the syllable divisions. The pencil or finger also assists the student in keeping his or her eyes moving from left to right along the line of print. This procedure can help the student who skips or confuses word parts to focis more securely upon the symbol patterns from the beginning to the end of a word.

2. When reading, the student should be required to sound aloud all words which are difficult, but involve units already introduced. The teacher should provide any words or parts of words that have not yet been taught.

3. The teacher should supply the student with lists of appropriate words for practicing newly taught units or those still causing difficulty. When unsure of a word, the student should underline the vowel patterns, place a dot where each syllable division might occur, determine the vowel sounds, and blend the syllables together to decode the word. The teacher needs to devise a method for keeping track of the student's errors, confusions, or hesitations in order to know which elements need continued review.

The following list gives an idea of what might be included in a practice list for a student beginning to learn syllable patterns and division rules. The list would look like this to the student:

silent	pentathlon
tripod	verbal
different	combination

When the student is through with such a list, his/her paper should look like this:

si.lent	pen.tath.lon
tri.pod	ver.bal
dif.fer.ent	com.bin.a.tion

Continuum for working with language skills

The following illustration of the language continuum will help the teacher keep in mind an overview of most language components. The notations used on this continuum are sequenced from left to right, generally ordered from simple to more complex. More discussion of the logic of each of these sequences can be found later in this manual.

Sounds and Word Units

a	f	er	str	-ing	-tion	per-	-ology	cious

Syllables

C	L	O	V	E	R
Closed	Consonant-le	Open	Vowel team	Vowel-consonant-e	r controlled

Syllable Division Rules

#1	#2	#3	#4	#5	#6	#7
vc.cv	v.cv	vc.v	.cle	v.v	word.word	prefix.root.suffix

Adding Suffixes

1	2	3	4
Just add	double for short vowel	words ending in -e	words ending in -y

Prefixes

phonetically regular	consistent but schwaed	chameleon groups	multiple spellings

Suffixes

phonetically regular	consistent but schwaed		multiple spellings

Roots

fix	port	tract	mit miss	script scribe	ceed cede, cess	cycl

Parts of Speech

nouns	adjectives	verbs	adverbs	prepositions	conjunctions

It is linguistically illogical to teach one complete segment of the continuum before going on to another; for example, do not teach all of the prefixes before going on to suffixes. If the student knows the short vowel sounds securely, the teacher can introduce closed syllable prefixes and root words, and then teach the VC.CV syllable division rule before going on to open syllables and other syllable division rules. If the student does not know the short vowel sounds, the teacher should use the following sequence: the open syllable pattern, with the familiar long vowel sound (same as the letter name); the vowel-consonant-e syllable pattern, also with the familiar long vowel sounds; and then the rule applied when adding suffixes to words ending with -e. At the same time, the teacher can gradually introduce the short vowel sounds, one at a time, allowing practice with each one to assure mastery. Prefixes and root words using the short vowel sound introduced provide excellent practice material.

The following resource list provides the teacher with some of the many reference materials which can be helpful:

Steere, Amy. *Solving Language Difficulties*. Cambridge, MA: Educators Publishing Service, Inc., 1996.

Henry, Marcia. *Words*. Austin, TX: PRO-Ed. Novato, CA: Academic Therapy Publications, 1990.

Bowen, Carolyn. *Angling for Words*, TX: PRO-Ed. Novato, CA: Academic Therapy Publications, 1972.

Greene, Amsel. *Word Clues: The Vocabulary Builder*. Blacklick, Ohio: Glencoe, 1984.

Ehrlich, Ida. *Instant Vocabulary*. New York, NY: Pocket Books, Simon & Schuster, Inc., 1968.

Prefixes . . . a resource book; Suffixes . . . a resource book; Roots . . . a resource book. Cooper, Follis, Lindsay, and Parsons, Tantalus Research Limited. Vancouver, B.C., V7H 1Z7.

Plunkett, Mildred B. *A Spelling Workbook Emphasizing Rules and Generalizations for Corrective Drill*. Cambridge, MA: Educators Publishing Service, Inc., 1966.

Rudd, Josephine. *Word Attack Manual*. Cambridge, MA: Educators Publishing Service, Inc., 1996.

8. PROCEDURES FOR TEACHING SPELLING

There is a series of steps for teaching spelling which assures that the student is fully utilizing a multisensory approach, as well as using the information which has been taught concerning the structure of the English language. Whether the teacher is dictating words, phrases, or sentences to be written, the procedures are similar. They are as follows:

1. The teacher dictates the material while enunciating clearly, but not over-pronouncing sounds, or separating longer words into syllables.

2. The student must repeat the dictation aloud at least once and sometimes two or three times if necessary. This allows auditory feedback from the student's **own** voice and kinesthetic feedback cues from the student's **own** speech musculature when she/he is pronouncing. Repetition, combined with the auditory and kinesthetic reinforcement, will aid in the retention of dictated material. It will also reveal to the teacher whether the student is pronouncing and has remembered the word(s) correctly.

3. For single word dictation or for longer words included in phrases and sentences, the student must be able to break the word into syllables. The student with minor problems may only need to sound each syllable aloud as it is written. The student with more serious problems may need to use the fingers of the nonwriting hand to count the number of syllables before writing. This provides another visual and kinesthetic memory device which can help the student to write something on paper representing each spoken syllable.

   When spelling skills improve, finger counting of syllables, if it has been used, may be eliminated or utilized only when the student realizes that he/she is having a problem with a word. It also is helpful for the student to determine, if possible, the root word within the long word. The teacher must remain aware that spoken syllable patterns may sometimes differ from the syllable notations in a dictionary. For example, the word 'definition' may be divided orally as (def - in - i - tion) while the dictionary division is often indicated as (def - i- ni - tion).

4. The student then writes what has been dictated, sounding aloud while writing. Only by sounding aloud can a student fully benefit from feedback from his/her own kinesthetic mouth clues and auditory processing system. The student with severe dyslexia will usually need to separate the sounds within a syllable, and pronounce each one aloud while writing. A student with a milder problem will need to separate a syllable into separate sounds only when the complete syllable is causing difficulty.

5. After completing the dictation, the student reads aloud what has been written. For almost all dyslexic students, the visual recognition of words is more secure than the recall of symbols needed for writing them. In order to utilize this strength, the student is taught to go back and read aloud what he/she has actually written; sometimes this is quite different from what he/she intended to write. Editing one's own writing presents a problem for many people. However, for those with the added factor of an insecure visual memory for words, this creates a double jeopardy. The student must be taught to reread work as carefully as possible, checking any questionable words in the dictionary or on the computer spell check when writing papers for school.

6. If a student is using a pencil with an eraser, the teacher must be aware that having dyslexia often makes it difficult to recognize errors created by erasing and altering a written word. While doing written work, the student corrects any recognized errors, rewriting the entire word rather than erasing and substitut-

ing other letters. If a student uses a pen during each lesson, it provides the teacher with a record of confusions and uncertainties. It also prevents the student from erasing too many letters or not enough letters, thereby making a new error. It provides more reinforcement for the student to resequence and write rather than "patch" mistakes, and it saves time. When uncertain if an error was made, the student should underline the word or areas within the word which are suspect. What the teacher does with the spelling errors (those self-corrected and those unrecognized) will depend largely upon the primary purpose of that spelling lesson. If not dealt with at that time, the error should be noted; the teacher can include ways to deal with the uncertainty in a later lesson plan. Two suggestions are:

(a) Reinforcing a newly introduced word unit or rule by having the student rewrite any word which has caused difficulty once or twice, and then writing several other words which contain that same spelling pattern.

(b) Analyzing the student's error patterns and confusions, and planning an appropriate review list of words for the spelling portion of the next lesson(s). When the same confusions continue to occur, the teacher may need to go back and redo the steps of introducing the sound, affix, or rule in order to assure mastery.

Spelling errors generally fall into four categories:

1. Addition or omission of sounds or letters (begain/began; proffessor/professor; compition/competition; statician/statistician). The teacher asks the student to read what has actually been written. If this does not help him/her find the error, the teacher then asks the student to trace the letters written and to sound aloud what his/her hand is tracing and actually writing.

2. Transposition of letter order (three/there; yellow/yollew; church/chruch; perdict/predict). The teacher does the same as for errors noted in #1.

3. Incorrect spelling choice (avoid/avoyed; blue/blew; jealous/jelous; schedule/schedual; politition/politician; loneliness/lonlyness). If the student is able to recognize that an incorrect spelling choice has been made, the teacher asks the student to isolate the sound and write down all the possibilities of spelling the sound that he/she knows. If the student cannot recognize the error, the teacher indicates the problem area by underlining or circling it. The student then isolates the sound needed, writes the known multiple spelling possibilities for that sound, crosses out those that will not apply for some reason, (ex. final position spelling for a mid-word sound) and tries writing the word with another spelling choice.

4. Failure to apply a spelling rule or generalization (furry/fury; immediately/immediatly; acquaint/aquaint; committing/commiting). In some cases the teacher would only need to ask the student to read exactly what has been written. In doing so he/she might recognize the error. In other situations, (studied/studyed) only the oral recall of the rule may help the student determine the error. Once the correct spelling has been chosen, the word should be rewritten correctly several times. A number of other words using the same pattern as the one confused should be dictated, either immediately or during succeeding lessons, to reinforce the correct choice.

From time to time, in the spelling portion of lessons, the teacher will want to ask the student for a creative writing sample. The procedures the student follows are the same as those for dictation except he/she will be choosing the vocabulary. Sounding aloud and self-editing procedures will always be important parts of such an exercise, and with continued practice the student will eventually master the language units which persist in being difficult.

Much of the teaching of dyslexic students involves challenging their thinking about the structure of words and word patterns, and analyzing what letter patterns should or might be used in certain positions in a word. For example, -i- and -ie- are used in the middle of words while -y- and -ey are usually used in the final position. It helps to know some of the history of our language, and that words have origins with different levels of complexity. For example, roots of Anglo-Saxon origin involve short vowel signals such as -ck (backing), -tch (pitcher), -dge (dodged), -ll (filling), -ff (fluffy), and -ss (messes), etc. Roots of Latin origin ending in -ct- expand into tion (act/action). Words from the Greek use ph for (f), ch for (k), and y for (long or short -i-). They are often found together in the same word (psychic, synchronize). The teacher can direct the student's thinking by the type of questions asked. The question must make the student focus on the element of language needed to solve the dilemma about a word. For example, if the student writes "glumey" or "glume" for gloomy, or "compition" for competition, the teacher can ask, "What is the root word?" If the student is able to decide the root for gloomy, then it may become clear that the word is extended from the root word "gloom' with the suffix -y- added. Asked the same question about competition, the student can realize that the word builds from the word "compete," with the final e dropped and the suffix -ition added. Thinking about words in this way will gradually teach the student how to analyze advanced vocabulary. Through experience and greater familiarity with language structure and rules, a teacher will gain skill in selecting appropriate questions.

Over a period of time, the teacher must include some work on common nonphonetic words, which do not follow the spelling rules or generalizations covering most words. These words should be introduced a few at a time, adjusting the number to fit each student's ability to memorize the words. The older student should be given the responsibility of studying them independently, so as not to take up valuable lesson time. Because these words need to be learned by rote, they are learned more securely if the student says the *letter names* aloud while writing them. Simultaneous hand movement and speech production provide the student with the best possible multisensory reinforcement. Frequent review is necessary. A list of these words can be found on page 57. An effort has been made to list them in order of frequency of use to help the teacher decide the order in which to introduce these nonphonetic words.

9. SYLLABLE PATTERNS AND SYLLABLE DIVISION RULES

Students who experience difficulty with advanced vocabulary often have not learned about syllable patterns and the role syllable patterns play in analyzing words. When the teacher can simplify and organize this area of language structure, a greater independence in reading and writing polysyllabic words will develop.

Though not found in any dictionary, an easy definition of a syllable is, "A vowel pattern and the consonants that go with it." The student will need help at first to understand what is meant by ". . . that go with it." All words in our language can be grouped into six syllable types; all but one center around a vowel pattern which represents a speech sound. Just learning this can be reassuring to a student who has not mastered the mystery of the English language. The syllable patterns are as follows:

C —

closed: has one vowel at the beginning or in the middle of the syllable, which usually has a short sound. In an unaccented syllable, the vowel may have a schwaed sound (see reference for schwa, page 32) (at, cat, scat, scratch, it, fit, strip, ad-, trans-, -tact-, -dict-, speck, in<u>struct</u>, con<u>trast</u>, <u>chron</u>ology, foo<u>lish</u>)

L —

consonant-le: usually the final syllable of a word. The only syllable pattern in which the vowel does not make a sound (-ble, -cle, -ckle, -dle, -fle, -gle, -ple, -tle, -zle, -stle)

bram<u>ble</u>	un<u>cle</u>	arti<u>cle</u>	tri<u>ckle</u>	mishan<u>dle</u>
ri<u>fle</u>	wri<u>ggle</u>	ma<u>ple</u>	unset<u>tle</u>	puz<u>zle</u>
nee<u>dle</u>	trou<u>ble</u>	cas<u>tle</u>	poss<u>ible</u>	sylla<u>ble</u>

O —

open: has one vowel at the end of the syllable, which usually has a long sound. In an unaccented syllable, the vowel may have its schwaed sound (see reference for schwa, page 32)

me	hi	go	<u>tri</u>pod	<u>de</u>fend
<u>pro</u>mote	<u>re</u>view	<u>si</u>lent	<u>cu</u>bic	<u>vi</u>brate
<u>spo</u>ken	<u>pa</u>tient	<u>flu</u>ently	<u>pli</u>able	<u>mu</u>tual

V —

vowel team: has two vowels together that usually make just one vowel sound (ee, ea, oi, ou, oa, au, aw, oy, eu, ow, ew, etc.)

feet	stream	spoil	ouch	float	saw	blow	shoot
rain	found	feud	<u>sau</u>nter	re<u>new</u>al		refe<u>ree</u>	

(Note: in this pattern -w combines with the a, e, and o to represent a vowel sound.)

E —

vowel-consonant-e: first vowel usually has its long sound (-ite, -ope, -ube, -ade, -eve, -ane, -ize, -ate, -ile, etc.)

strike	spoke	trade	sphere	per<u>vade</u>	pre<u>cise</u>

(Note: consonant digraphs function as one consonant — bathe, clothe, ache)

R —

r controlled: all the vowels combined with r

er	ir	ur	ar	or	-or	-ar	ear	yr
her	third	purse	sharp	porch	doc<u>tor</u>	po<u>lar</u>	earth	mart<u>yr</u>

(Note: second –or and –ar are suffix examples.)

Some language reference books, spelling workbooks, etc., make reference to seven syllables. The authors of these materials consider certain vowel patterns listed in the vowel team group to be diphthongs that have two distinct speech sounds blended together very quickly. Many people think of diphthongs as a single sound, among them oi, au, and ow. Dyslexic students need language information to be simplified as much as possible. It does not create problems for them to think of the diphthongs as vowel teams. The rare exception to this might be when they are doing workbook pages in a spelling or English class and are expected to make the fine distinction between vowel teams and diphthongs.

The more severely language impaired student will need to learn these syllable patterns one at a time, practicing them in isolation, just as a younger student needs to learn a new sound unit in isolation before combining it with others. A student with more advanced language skills can be shown all six patterns required to be studied, though the teacher should still plan practice sessions on just one pattern at a time. For practice, the prefix and root card decks can be separated into the various syllable patterns and used for both visual and auditory drill work with syllables. Lists of the syllables can also be used for practice. During lesson time, the student should also be given a list of polysyllabic words and asked to underline the vowel patterns within the syllables. The words chosen should involve only those syllable patterns which have already been taught. As new syllable patterns are introduced, the number expands until all are mastered. For example, the student should learn to underline as follows: (planet, vacant, sleepy, maintain, protractor, modernize ,brittle). Note the different underlining used with the consonant-le syllable in brittle. We have found that underlining all three letters reinforces the concept of this unusual syllable; doing this helps the student determine the pronunciation of the vowel preceding the syllable.

When working on this task, the question may arise about what to do with the vowel pattern in syllables such as -tion and -sion. Even though the -io- is not a vowel team and the i is really serving to indicate the (sh) sound for the t or the (sh/zh) sound for the s, it seems easiest at first to teach that the -io- can be underlined as a maverick vowel team. The other question which arises relates to what the student should do about the final -e in words such as goose, attendance, or large. The letter -e does not make a sound nor does it indicate a syllable pattern, but rather it serves as a linguistic "signal" keeping a word from looking like a plural form or indicating that c be read as (s), or a g read as (j). The student should underline the -e at first glance. After learning that the e is serving as a "signal," rather than a syllable "indicator," the student can put a slash (/) through the line written under the e. For example, (goose, large). Later, when the student has been taught the other functions of final e, this procedure for dealing with its special pattern begins to make sense and creates little if any confusion.

Unlike book publishers or newspaper editors, students with dyslexia can avoid having to divide syllables at the end of a line. When individuals who are secure with reading are unsure of the division of a word, they move to the beginning of the next line and write the word there, eliminating the need to remember where the syllables divide. The dyslexic student can do the same. However, syllable patterns and syllable division rules are particularly important for the dyslexic, for it enables them to:

1. Break longer words into smaller, more manageable speech units. The shorter units are more easily analyzed, pronounced, reviewed and blended back together for ordering speech sounds to read words or for sequencing patterns for spelling.

2. Determine whether the single-letter vowel comes in the middle or at the end of the syllable. Knowing this is essential to deciding whether the vowel should be read as a long or short sound. This knowledge will usually help a student to determine spelling patterns as well. For example, a single vowel among consonants may be read with its short or long sound; which is used depends entirely upon its place in the syllable. A student can be taught to reason that, when changing the word (hop) to (hopping), the final (p) needs to be doubled (hop.ping) in order to protect the short vowel sound in the root. A second (p) directs the reader to divide the syllable between the two (p's) and read the first syllable as a closed syllable with the vowel given its short sound. When the student wants to change the word (hope) to (hop-

ing), he/she must drop the final e̲, which served as the signal for the long sound for o̲ before adding -ing, a suffix which starts with a vowel. With the -e̲ dropped, the base word still has only one (p), and the suffix can be added. The word becomes a two syllable one requiring a division. In the thousands of words with this pattern, the syllable division becomes V.CV indicating that the first syllable is now an open syllable. The writer has simply replaced one long vowel signal for a different long vowel signal.

As mentioned before, the indication of the syllable division shown in the dictionary is not always helpful for the dyslexic. For example, when adding (ing) to the root word 'hope,' the final e̲ is dropped; most dictionaries would indicate the syllable division for the word 'hoping' as hop.ing, leaving the remaining letters of the root together. For the student with a reading difficulty, it is easier to think of the division as ho.ping because it helps maintain the long sound for the o̲. The teacher can think of these division rules as "vowel sound determiners" and explain to a student why this division is in conflict with the dictionary syllable division rules.

The pronunciation of vowels in other syllables such as consonant-le, v-e, and vowel teams is determined by language rules and word origins. In a very few words, there are no clear cut rules which will help a student decide which pronunciation is needed. Consider for example, the final syllable -ine which can sound three different ways; (-īn) as in pi̲ne, (ēn) as in magazi̲ne, (ən) as in femini̲ne.

The pronunciation of a single vowel between consonants is determined by its position within its own syllable. A vowel at the beginning or in the middle of a syllable usually is read with its short sound and the vowel that comes at the end of a syllable is usually read with its long sound. Again, the indication of the syllable division shown in the dictionary is not always helpful for the dyslexic. For example, most dictionaries would indicate the syllable division for the word 'taking' as tak.ing. For the student with a reading difficulty, it would be easier to think of the division as ta.king.

Syllable Division Rules

In this section the following abbreviations apply: V = vowel; C = consonant; (.) = division location (to eliminate visual clutter, we recommend a dot (.) be used to mark the division break rather than the traditional slash (/).) The seven basic division patterns are listed below. (The order in which these division rules are taught can be varied according to the student's need.)

1.	**V C.C V**	**V C. C C V**	**VC.CCCV**	**V C C .CC V**	**VCCC.CV**
	mu̲f.fi̲n	in.tro̲.du̲ce	in.struct	trans.pla̲nt	patch.wo̲rk
	pla̲s.ti̲c	ba̲sh.fu̲l	ci̲r.cu̲m.scri̲be	wi̲th.sta̲nd.ing	

With these patterns, the division comes between two of the consonants following the first vowel pattern. When this occurs, it creates a closed syllable with a short vowel sound before the division point. This division never determines the sound of the vowel which follows the division point. That vowel's pronunciation will be determined only by the division of the letters in the next syllable.

2. & 3.	**V. C V**	**V C. V**
	o̲.pen	li̲m.i̲t
	smi̲.ling	pa̲n.e̲l

This pattern has two possibilities that the student needs to be taught. The V.C V division occurs more frequently and should be introduced first. This allows continuation in a left to right progression across the word, a procedure to be encouraged with a dyslexic student whenever possible. The V.CV division creates an open syllable which usually indicates a long vowel sound.

If dividing V.CV does not produce a word which sounds familiar, the student is taught to move the division after the consonant VC.V, creating a closed syllable with a short vowel sound (cab.in; bu.col.ic; rev.o.lu.tion). If neither maneuver creates a familiar word, the student needs to check the dictionary or ask someone for help. Once the concept of accent and schwa is taught, then the student can apply that information to help decode an unfamiliar word.

4. .cle

This syllable pattern requires special attention because it is the only one that does not have a vowel sound. In this pattern, the initial consonant and the l always stay together, and the final -e does not sound (bub.ble, han.dle). If there is a vowel just before the division point, the vowel will have its long sound (bu.gle, cra.dle). If there is a consonant before the division point, the vowel will be closed in and will have its short sound (rid.dle, bat.tle).

There are two consonant-le patterns that also need special attention (-ckle and -stle). Some dictionaries indicate the syllable division for -ckle should come between the k and the le (pick.le). If the student knows that -ck always follows a short vowel sound, this division will not create a reading or spelling problem. In -stle (sounded as sl), the t is silent; dictionaries indicate the division between the s and the t (cas.tle). This does not present a problem for determining the pronunciation of the vowel before -stle, because the s will close in the vowel and indicate its short sound (whis.tle; tres.tle).

5. V.V

Sometimes two vowels which are not vowel teams come together in words (ia, eo, iu, etc.). The syllable division will come between them, indicating the first vowel as an open syllable with a long vowel sound.

di.a.logue	hid.e.ous	tri.umph	cha.ot.ic

Occasionally, vowels come together that look like vowel teams but do not function that way (ea, oi, ui, etc.). They, too, are divided and the first vowel in the combination is usually long.

cre.a.tion	e.go.ist	flu.id

6. word.word

In compound words, when the two combined and identifiable words are separated, each sound as if they were standing alone.

house.boat	cow.boy	nurse.maid	play.mate

7. prefix . root . suffix

pro.mote	inter.rupt.ed	auto.bio.graph.ically

When a student has learned prefix, root, and suffix units in isolation, they are ready to divide longer words. There is no need to separate such units as auto-, tele-, -ology, or -ically into their separate syllables unless the dyslexic student is momentarily unsure of how to read one of them. The affixes and roots divide into syllable patterns listed under number(s) 1 and/or 2. Most often the affixes can be separated from the root word for analyzing (ex: in.con.ceiv.able; myth.ology; non.inter.ven.tion).

The teacher needs to plan for special work on the prefixes that are in the open syllable group (re-, pre-, pro-, tri-, etc.) but when joined to some roots, become VC.V patterns and closed syllables instead. For example, consider:

re.volve - rev.olution	pre.pare - prep.aration
pro.pose - prop.osition	de.fine - def.inition

The above patterns are numbered to clarify the concepts for the teacher. It is imperative that the student understands how syllable division patterns work and their effect on vowel sounds. However, there is no need to think in terms of the rule number or pattern being used. For example, the word 'contractor' can be divided as con.trac.tor (applying #1) or con.tract.or (applying #4); in both situations the pronunciation of the word will be the same, and the rule number applied is inconsequential. EPS has excellent resource materials to use for practicing syllabication, such as *Solving Language Difficulties* by Amy Steere, Caroline Peck, and Linda Kahn. The gradual mastery of this information opens an entirely new way of looking at words. As one adult who had been illiterate said, after working on language in this way, "When I used to look at words, they were just a jumble of letters that made no sense. Now when I look at words, they just fall apart." When questioned further, he said, "They fall into prefixes, roots, and suffixes."

10. ACCENT AND SCHWA

Older students working with multisyllabic words need to learn about accenting syllables and the schwaed sounds of single vowels and vowels in some of the r-controlled syllables. These are rather complicated concepts for many and may take time to master.

A single vowel can have a long vowel sound if it comes at the end of its syllable (va.ca.tion), a short vowel sound if it comes at the beginning or middle of the syllable (am.ple, mag.nify), or the schwaed sound (den.tal). This shift in pronunciation does not occur with vowel teams since they usually have only one sound. Also, the sound they represent in a word is not determined by their placement in the syllable, as the single vowels are. For example, ee will have the sound of long ($\bar{e}$) and ai will have the sound of long ($\bar{a}$) no matter where they occur in words.

The rules concerning accenting syllables are not always regular and consistent, causing some difficulty for the student with a reading problem. There are a few rules that govern concepts and patterns that can be taught. For these suggestions, see Accent Placement Rules on page 68.

The schwa sound occurs when a vowel appears in an unaccented syllable. Dealing with spelling the schwaed sound of vowels presents a problem because all the vowels, when schwaed, sound the same. The pronunciation varies, sounding somewhere between short u (as in up) to the e in competition, i in confident, to almost no sound at all, as in the a in mental. Learning the pronunciations and spellings for affix and root patterns provides a good deal of help. To know there are two ways to spell the prefix (əp-) (ap- and op-) and five different ways to spell the suffix (-ən) (-en, -an, -on, -ain, -ine) aids the student. Adding to that, the knowledge of meanings and derivations helps. For example: ap- means to or toward (approach, appeal); op- means away from (oppose); -en comes at the ends of Anglo-saxon roots (eaten, hidden, stolen, forgotten); -an is used to indicate people (custodian, comedian, American); -on has no clear meaning, but is the next most commonly used (season, button), -ain is the next-best guess (mountain, captain); -ine is rare (engine).

To teach the concept of schwa, the teacher starts with two syllable words well known to the student, such as rabbit and mitten. The student should be asked to underline the vowel patterns and mark the syllable divisions (rab.bit, mit.ten). When asked to pronounce the first syllable all by itself, as though it were a word, the student should be able to hear the a in rabbit clearly sounds as (ă). The teacher could put the breve (˘) over the a. When the student pronounces the second syllable in isolation, as it sounds in the word, she/he should be able to hear that the vowel i is schwaed, e.g., (bət). The vowel can be crossed through with a light x. Do the same for mit.ten; the first syllable is mĭt, the vowel sounds clearly and is marked with a (˘), the second syllable is pronounced (tən) and the e is crossed through with an x. The word printed on the page would look like (răb′bīt) or (mĭt′tĕn). After exposure to many such words, the student begins to hear the clear vowel sounds and the schwaed or indistinct vowel pronunciations. An accent mark can be placed at the end of the syllable, and the impact the accent has on the vowel pronunciation can be discussed and the word pronounced. When this concept is learned, the student can apply it to any word that is not immediately recognized. Words which build from the same root but have accent changes can be studied to further aid in understanding how helpful this can be for reading, spelling, and pronunciation (civ′əl, civ′əl.ize, cə.vil′ian). This enables them to eventually pronounce challenging words such as ratiocination or discombobulation.

11. LESSON PLANNING

Effective organization of information for a student working at the higher level of the English language presents a challenge. Planning for lessons, remembering what has been introduced, keeping track of the student's confusions, and what needs further review are essential to language instruction that is carefully sequenced and structured. It is particularly challenging because the teacher needs to introduce a mixture of new rules, affixes, and root words rather than introduce all of the prefixes before moving on to root words and then on to suffixes. With this in mind, the teacher needs to find an efficient way to track a good deal of information.

An effort should be made to divide the lesson period into thirds:

1. One-third for drill work and introduction of new material.

2. One-third for spelling and writing.

3. One-third for oral reading of word lists and phrases, sentences, fictional narrative or text books.

Lesson plans help the teacher use the time with the student efficiently; the teacher can detour when the need or opportunity arises and then return to the main track. If the lesson plan is written in pencil or pen, notations about the errors and confusions can be made in colored ink. This makes it easy to see at a glance what needs to be included as review in subsequent lessons. The plan also provides an excellent logbook to be used for conferences with students, parents and other teachers. Keep them, for they can provide information necessary for staffing, can give a student some idea of what has been covered, and can be used as a date record by a private tutor for billing purposes.

When working with advanced language, the teacher must handle a number of language concepts simultaneously. A lesson plan with information and explanations can be found on the next page. Frequent review of previously taught material must be included in the lessons. One efficient way to help with this process is to compile a loose-leaf notebook for each student to keep, with divisions for each of the essential areas: (1) basic language structure (including any phonic sounds, rules, and multiple spellings as they are introduced), (2) rules for advanced language, (3) multiple spellings of prefixes, (4) multiple spellings of suffixes, (5) syllable patterns and syllable division rules, (6) prefixes, (7) suffixes, (8) connectives, (9) root words, (10) parts of speech/grammar; (11) student's writing samples.

New information presented can be written on a page and put in the front of the notebook. When the student opens the notebook, the pages coming before the first divider will serve as a reminder of the material needing to be studied. The pages may include material taught earlier, which is still causing confusions and needs to be reviewed, along with the most recently introduced material still needing practice for mastery. As concepts are securely learned, page(s) can be filed behind the appropriate divider. If review of material taught previously is needed, related pages can be moved to the front of the notebook as a reminder for the student and the teacher. When such a notebook is maintained, the student will have a ready reference for information. It will facilitate review work when parents, friends, or other teachers wish to help. First and foremost, it needs to be kept in mind that the student needs to understand the information and how it fits into what already has been learned about "how the English language works." A well organized and informative notebook can be used as a tool to help the student learn, a *means* to an important end, and *not* an end in itself.

Lesson Plan for Advanced Student

Name: _____   Lesson # ____

Date: _____

Note: There is no separate notation for kinesthetic drills. Kinesthetic reinforcement, provided by the student's hand-arm and speech musculature feel and movement, should routinely be incorporated into every aspect of the lesson.

Note: The term 'Basic,' under the Visual and Auditory Drills, applies to elementary phonics and language structure; such as those found in the *Language Tool Kit* and other similar materials.

Review: Old Review: any elements that are not securely learned or any confusion resulting
                     from a segment of a recent lesson
                     New Review: the sounds/rules/generalizations/concepts which were just introduced

Visual drill: go over whatever is appropriate for the student, considering age and level of language
                     functioning, and what has been introduced
                     Basics — Prefixes — Suffixes — Roots

Auditory drill: would be the same as for the visual drill
                     Basics — Prefixes — Suffixes — Roots

Blending drill: sounds, phrases, words, (real or nonsense syllables)

Introduction of new material: when the student seems ready, introduce a new sound unit,
                     word unit, rule, generalization

Spelling: review of new or recently taught information or elements which requires more reinforcement
                     and practice; may include word lists, phrases, sentences, student's spontaneous writing with
                     self-editing

Reading: practice those language units being learned or needing review
                     Material: _____ page #____
                     may include word lists, phrases, sentences, newspaper or magazine articles, stories, or books

Non-phonetic: review of some of the non-phonetic words learned and/or addition of one or two new ones

Homework: assign something appropriate related to rules, roots, affixes, or non-phonetic words introduced;
                     something written and edited by student before coming to class

Summary: talk about what has been covered during this lesson; have student summarize whenever
                     possible

                     (Note: See Appendix for outline version which can be reproduced.)

34

12. PREFIXES

I.   Introduction to Prefixes

The following diagram provides an overview of the progression used in teaching prefixes:

phonetically regular	schwaed	chameleon groups	multiple spellings

Closed syllable prefixes have two pronunciation possibilities. When they are accented, the vowel is usually pronounced with its short sound. When the syllable is unaccented, the vowel sound may be schwaed (*com´.ple.ment, com.plain´*). The vowel in an open syllable prefix has three possible pronunciations; long, short or schwaed (*pre´.mature, pred´.icate, pre.fer´*). Prefixes consisting of two syllables may have varying pronunciation possibilities, since they may be made up of open or closed syllables. The accent may shift from one of the syllables to the other depending upon the root and the suffixes which are added (*ge´.o.graph´.ic, ge.og´.ra.phy´*). The general pattern presented below will help the teacher present prefixes in a logical order.

Some prefixes are almost always pronounced phonetically. They are as follows:

open syllable	closed syllable		r control
bi-	dif-	sub-	counter-
co-	dis-	suc-	for-
contra-	dys-	suf-	fore-
intra-	em-	sum-	inter-
intro-	en-	sup-	over-
multi-	il-	sus-	per-
tri-	im-	syl-	super-
uni-	in-	sym-	sur-
	mid-	syn-	ir-
	mis-	trans-	hyper-
	non-	un-	para-
	pan-	with-	out-

Other prefixes have two pronunciations. They are the short vowel sound and the schwaed sound (*as´set, as.sist´*). Still others have three pronunciations. They are the long vowel, the short vowel, or the schwaed sound (*e.vict´, ev´ident, e.rase´*). Included in this second group are the following:

Closed	Open	Other patterns
Short vowel sound	Long vowel sound	
Schwaed	Short vowel sound	
	Schwaed	be-
		cor-
ab-		post-
ac-	a-	al-
ad-	de-	
af-	di-	
ag-	e-	
al-	pre-	
an-	pro-	
ap-	re-	
ar-	se-	
as-		
at-		
col-		
com-		
con-		
ef-		
ex-		
mal-		
ob-		
oc-		
op-		
an.ti-		
cir.cum- (also r controlled)		
sem.i-		

A number of two syllable prefixes which are combinations of different syllable patterns have varying pronunciations, depending upon the placement of the accent. The accent can change according to the root word and/or the suffix added (*tel´e.graph, tel.eg´raph.er, mon´o.logue, mon.op´oly*). The following are the prefixes included in this group:

Two Syllable Patterns with Changes of Pronunciation

ante-	anti-	epi-	equi-
auto-	geo-	homo-	hypo-
micro-	mono-	photo-	psycho-
dia-	poly-	semi-	tele-
circum-			

The prefixes in all the above groups are listed alphabetically; however, they do not need to be presented in that order. Generally, one-syllable prefixes are introduced before those with two syllables; those that are phonetically regular or are pronounced in a consistent way are presented before those with shifting accent possibilities.

II.   Supplementary List–Prefixes

The Latin and Greek prefixes or combining forms listed below are not common enough to warrant inclusion in the card deck. However, a teacher working with a bright high school or college student, or an adult, may want to include them, since they are a part of the advanced vocabulary which the student may need. Though they are listed in alphabetical order, the teacher should select the units that seem appropriate for the student being taught. In some, a variation of spelling occurs.

Prefix	Examples	Meaning
aero-	aerodynamics, aeriform, aerate	air
ambi-	ambidextrous, ambiguous, ambivalent	both
ana-	analysis, anatomy, anathema	up, against
apo-	apostle, apology, apocryphal	away, different from
aqua-	aquaplane, aqueduct, aquatic	water
bene-	benefit, benefactor, beneficial	well
bio-	biophysics, biology, biography	life
cata-	catacomb, catastrophe, catapult	downward, against
cent-	centigrade, centipede, bicentennial	hundred
dec-	decade, decimal, decathlon	ten
ec-	eccentric, eclipse, ecstasy (variation of ex-)	out of, from
eu-	eulogy, eugenics, euphony	good, well
extra-	extravagant, extraordinary, extrasensory	beyond, outside
helio-	helioscope, heliotropic, heliograph	sun
hemi-	hemisphere, hemicycle, hemiplegia	half
kilo-	kilocycle, kilowatt, kilogram	thousand
macro-	macrocosm, macrocephalic	large
manu-	manuscript, manufacture, manipulate	hand
mega-	megaphone, megaton, megalomania	large, great
meta-	metaphysical, metamorphosis, metastasize	after, along with
mill-	million, millimeter, millennium	thousand
mono-	monogram, monologue, monorail	one
neo-	neoclassic, Neolithic, neologism	new
novem-	November, novena	nine
oct-	octave, octagonal, octopus	eight
omni-	omnivorous, omniscient, omnipotent	all
pent-	pentagon, Pentecostal, pentathlon	five
peri-	periscope, perimeter, peripatetic	around
physi-	physical, physiology, physiotherapy	nature
pseudo-	pseudonym, pseudoclassic, pseudomorph	false, pretended
quad-	quadriplegic, quadruped, quadrangle	four
quar-	quarter, quartet, quartile	four

quasi-	quasi-official, quasi-serious quasi-controlled	resembling
quin(t)-	quintet, quintessence, quintuplet	five
retro-	retroactive, retrospect, retrograde	backward
sept-	septate, September, septillion	seven
sex-	sextet, sextant, sexagenarian	six
stereo-	stereophonic, stereotype, stereoscopic	solid
theo-	theocratic, theology, atheist	God
ultra-	ultrasonic, ultramodern, ultraviolet	beyond

III.   Multiple Spelling Choices–Prefixes

Because prefixes are sometimes the unaccented syllable, and thus have schwaed vowel sounds, a few multiple spelling possibilities occur. A student will need to learn the following multiples in order to make correct spelling choices:

a-	(on, in, up, out, etc.)	e- (out)	
	away		event
	ago		evict
	around		elaborate
	amid		elect
ac-	(to)	oc- (away from)	
	account		occur
	accord		occlude
	accuse		
	accredit		
ab-	(away)	ob- (away)	
	absolve		observe
	abrupt		obliterate
	abbreviate		object
	abrasive		oblige
ap-	(to)	op- (away)	
	appoint		oppose
	approve		oppress
	appear		oppugn
	applaud		
an-	(to, not)	un- (not)	
	annoy		unfeeling
	announce		unneeded
	annul		unnatural
	anachronism		undo

anti- (against)

    antifreeze

    antibody

    antisocial

    antiseptic

ante- (before)

    antechamber

    antedate

    antecedent

    antemeridium

---

de- (down, away)

    defend

    departure

    defect

    debate

di- (from, two)

    diminish

    divert

    diploma

    dilemma

---

dis- (not, negative)

    dislike

    disarm

    discord

    disservice

dys- (difficulty with)

    dyslexia

    dyscalculia

    dysgraphia

    dyspepsia

---

fore- (before)

    forehead

    forefathers

    foreword

    forewarn

for- (away)

    forget

    forgo

    forbid

    forsake

---

para- (beside)

    parallel

    paralegal

    paraphrase

    paraplegic

peri- (around)

    periscope

    peripatetic

    periodontal

    pericardium

---

pre- (before)

    predict

    prefer

    preside

    precocious

pro- (for)

    promote

    provide

    proposal

    propeller

13. SUFFIXES

I.   Introduction to Suffixes

The following diagram presents an overview of the progression used in teaching suffixes.

phonetically regular	consistent but schwaed	multiple spellings

Suffixes can be grouped into three basic categories:

1. Those that are consistent and phonetically regular (-ee, -ic, -oid).

2. Those that are consistent in their pronunciation but have the schwaed vowel sound (-able, -ity, -ment).

3. Those that have unexpected spellings or pronunciations inconsistent with previously learned sounds or patterns (-ed, -ward, -cian). Some suffixes have two pronunciations, one phonetically regular and one with the vowel schwaed (-ite – expedite, favorite; -ate – primate, private).

Because suffixes are usually unaccented syllables, the vowel sounds are often schwaed. This results in a number of suffixes which sound the same but are spelled differently (-ous, -us, -ess, -ice, -ant, -ent). Rules and generalizations for making spelling choices for suffixes are on page 42. This information can also be found on the cards accompanying the manual.

Many suffixes have just one spelling. First introduce those which are affixed to easier root words; often these are words of Anglo-Saxon origin (back<u>ing</u>, fool<u>ish</u>, slow<u>ly</u>). The teacher can then introduce suffixes which are pronounced regularly but are added to polysyllabic words with Latin and Greek roots (alt<u>itude</u>, nom-in<u>ee</u>, mus<u>ic</u>).

The suffixes are listed in a suggested order of presentation for the teacher's convenience, but flexibility is possible in the order in which these units are introduced. Whichever order is chosen, the teacher will need to find or create word lists that will provide the student with practice in reading and spelling words with the suffixes introduced.

List 1: Phonetically and consistently regular

-er	-ty	-tude	-eer
-ing	-ery	-id	-cle
-s	-ship	-hood	-crat
-y	-ize	-fold	-ese
-tion	-th	-most	-oid
-sion	-ic	-ster	-ule
-ation	-or	-ry	-mony
-ish	-ee	-ism	-osis
-ling	-ade	-cy	-fy
-ly			

List 2: Consistent but schwaed (*Note:* number notations refer to which pronunciation is being referred to on the back of the suffix card for this unit).

-ed (#1)	-es	-et	-est
-ment	-ful	-less	-ness
-some	-en	-ify	-ity
-age	-al	-ality	-ous
-able	-ess	-ical	-ible
-ar	-ant	-ance	-ate (#2)
-dom	-ent	-ence	-orous
-osity	-sis	-us	-ology
-ice	-cracy	-ure	-ory (#2)
-ine (#2)	-itis	-ite (#2)	-ile (#2)
-ard	-esce	-arity	-escence

(*Note:* Some of these combinations listed involve two or three suffixes, -ery, -ality, -arity, -ical, -ically, -orous.)

List 3: Unexpected pronunciations

-ed (#2 & #3)	-ive	-ture	-ary (#1 & #2)
-ward	-ette	-ically	-ability
-ian	-ior	-logue	-ial
-ion	-cial	-ious	-ium
-tious	-ine (#1)	-cious	-tial
-ibility			

II.　　**Rules for Adding Suffixes**

#1 Just add	#2 double for short vowel	#3 words ending in -e	#4 words ending in -y

#1.　When adding a suffix to root words, write the root word or the shorter, more familiar word, and add the suffix (*supplant – supplanted, convert – converter, tend – tending, mark – marker, detain – detaining, respect – respected*).

#2.　In a one-syllable word, with one short vowel ending in one consonant, double the final consonant before a suffix starting with a vowel (-ing, -er, -y, -ed, etc.). This will protect the short vowel (*strap – strapped, stop – stoppage, red – reddish*).
　　When adding a suffix to a two-syllable word, when the final syllable fits the pattern above, double the final consonant if the accent falls on the final syllable. This accent placement clearly makes the single vowel short, a sound that needs the protection of two consonants. If the final syllable is not accented, the vowel sound will be schwaed, and a schwaed vowel needs no protection (*remit´–remitting, combat´– combatting, propel´–propeller, forgot´–forgotten, but pock´eted, pi´loted, lim´iting*).

#3. When a root word ends in -e, a decision must be made whether to drop it or keep it:

Drop the final -e before a suffix beginning with a vowel (-ing, -ed, -able, -ous, etc.) (*debate – debated, mistake – mistaken, safe – safest, inspire – inspiration, fame – famous, intervene – intervening, active – activity*).

Keep the final -e before a suffix starting with a consonant (*sane – sanely, time – timeless, hope – hopeful, like – likeness, improve – improvement, safe – safety*).

A few words ending in -e do not fit these rules:

1. Keep final -e when it follows a soft c or g if the first letter of the suffix would cause their hard sound (*serviceable, advantageous*).
2. Keep final -e to protect the identity of the word (*singe – singeing* not *singing*, (*shoe – shoeing* not *shoing*)).

#4. When a root word ends in a -y, change the -y to an i before most suffixes (*try – tried – trial, roomy – roomier – roomiest, lonely – loneliness – lonelier*).

Keep final -y when:

1. the suffix starts with an i (-ing, -ist, -ish are the only suffixes needing to be considered) (*trying, emptying, lobbyist, babyish*).

2. the -y is part of a vowel team (ay, ey, oy).
(*play – played – playing – player – playful,
key – keyed – keying – keys,
enjoy – enjoyment – enjoying – enjoyed – enjoyable*).

A few words ending in y do not fit these rules:

(*dry – dryer, fly – flyer, say – said, pay – paid*).

III.   Multiple Spelling Choices

Because suffixes are often schwaed, some sound the same although they are spelled differently. Groups of suffixes with similar sounds are listed below. In general, the spellings in each group are listed in order of their frequency of occurrence. As with the prefixes, learning the meanings may help the student make some correct choices (-est = comparative; -ist = person). With other suffixes, applying the rules or generalizations will provide the answer (for soft c, use -ent as in innocent; for hard c, use -ant as in applicant). Mastery of the four basic parts of speech helps the student with some choices (-er used for comparative adjectives; -er and -or used for nouns, -ar used for adjectives). Knowing the root word is sometimes the only key to the correct suffix choice (face/facial, part/partial). There will be some choices for which the student will be unable to apply any linguistic "know how." The student can write the word using each possibility to see if one "looks correct"; if sill unable to decide by looking at the word, the dictionary will need to be consulted.

(ə-ble)	(shəs)	(əl)	(əd)
-able	-cious	-al	-ed
-ible	-tious	-el	-id
		-ile	

(ə-bǐl-ə-tē)	(er)	(shəl)	(əre)
-ability	-er	-cial	-ery
-ibility	-or	-tial	-ary
	-ar		-ory
	-ure		
			(ən)
(əns)	**(ənsē)**	**(əst)**	-en
-ance	-ancy	-est	-an
-ence	-ency	-ist	-on
			-ain
			-ine
(ənt)	**(əs)**	**(ət)**	
-ant	-ous	-et	
-ent	-ess	-ate	
	-us	-ite	**(ē)**
	-ice		-y
(shən)	**(ēən, yen)**		-ee
-tion	-ian		
-sion	-ion		
-cian			

IV.   Multiple Spellings With Examples

(-ə.bl´)

1. **-able** - (able; capable of)

   workable, eatable, unbeatable, forgettable
   [adjective suffix; usually added to a root that can stand alone as a
   recognizable word]

2. **-ible** - (able; capable of)

   edible, terrible, visible, compressible
   [adjective suffix; usually added to a root that does not stand alone
   as a recognizable word; added to a root word ending with -ss]

(ə.blē´)

1. **-ably** - (able; capable of)

   laughably, justifiably, believably, unavoidably
   [adverb suffix; variant form of -able; follows the same rules for usage]

2. **-ibly** - (able; capable of)

   possibly, audibly, forcibly, legibly
   [adverb suffix; variant form of -ible; follows the same rules for
   usage; used following soft c or g]

(ə.bǐ l.ə.tē)

1. **-ability** - (ableness)

   dependability, suitability, advisability, inexplicability
   [noun suffix; variant form of -able; follows the same rules for usage]

2. **-ibility** - (ableness)

   possibility, visibility, intelligibility, feasibility
   [noun suffix; variant form of -ible; follows the same rules for usage]

(ənt)

1. **-ant** - (one who; that pertaining to)

   attendant, consonant, indignant, arrogant
   [used after a root ending with hard c or g]

2. **-ent** - (one who; that pertaining to)

   fraudulent, magnificent, detergent, continent
   [used after a root ending with soft c or g]

(əns)

1. **-ance** - (state or quality of being)

   importance, reliance, significance, elegance,
   [noun suffix; used after a root ending with hard c or g]

2. **-ence** - (state or quality of being)

   difference, correspondence, magnificence, divergence
   [noun suffix; used after a root ending with soft c or g]

(əns.ē)

1. **-ancy** - (state or quality of being)

   vacancy, occupancy, pliancy, extravagancy
   [noun suffix; used after a root ending with hard c or g]

2. **-ency** - (state or quality of being)

   delinquency, emergency, pungency, despondency
   [noun suffix; used after a root ending with soft c or g]

44

(əl)

1. **-el** - (obscure)

   shovel, tunnel, bushel, barrel
   [usually a noun suffix; added to a root ending with <u>m</u>, <u>n</u>, <u>r</u>, <u>v</u>, <u>x</u>, <u>sh</u>]

2. **-al** - (pertaining to)

   dental, original, coastal, global
   [usually an adjective suffix; often added to a root from Latin]

3. **-ile** - (pertaining to)

   fertile, missile, facile, fragile
   [no specific grammar indicator; added to a root ending with soft <u>c</u> or <u>g</u>]

(ən)

1. **-en** - (past-tense action; varies)

   hidden, sweeten, forgiven, lighten, brazen
   [verb suffix; indicates action already completed; adjective suffix]

2. **-an** - (person; pertaining to)

   American, comedian, metropolitan, artisan
   [noun suffix; used to indicate a person; adjective suffix]

3. **-on** - (none)

   season, religion, region, million
   [noun suffix; actual suffix in -<u>tion</u>–action, -<u>sion</u>–tension units]

4. **-ain** - (obscure)

   captain, mountain, certain, Britain
   [usually a noun suffix]

5. **-ine** - (pertaining to; varies)

   feminine, masculine, medicine, engine
   [adjective and noun endings; added to a root ending with soft <u>c</u> or <u>g</u>]

(əs)

1. **-ous** - (full of; having)

   dangerous, fabulous, glorious, famous
   [common adjective suffix; added to Anglo-saxon and Latin roots]

2. **-ess** - (feminine ending)

   waitress, authoress, countess, goddess
   [noun suffix; used for words denoting a female]

3. **-us** - (obscure)

   bonus, minus, consensus, caucus
   [noun suffix; most often added to a Latin root]

4. **-ice** - (state or quality of)

   service, notice, novice, justice
   [usually noun suffix]

(əd)

1. **-ed** - (action already completed; past tense)

   wanted, blended, debated, corresponded
   [verb suffix; sounds as (-əd) following a root ending with the letter -t or -d]

2. **-id** - (having a quality; existence in a state)

   humid, torpid, limpid, frigid
   [adjective suffix]

(əst)

1. **-est** - (superlative; comparing three or more things)

   biggest, safest, happiest, brightest
   [adjective suffix; following Anglo-Saxon roots]

2. **-ist** - (one who)

   artist, dentist, optimist, columnist
   [noun suffix; used to indicate a person who does something]

(er)

1. **-er** - (one who is or that which does something; comparative)

   dancer, propeller, sillier, broader, alter
   [usually a noun suffix; indicates a person who or a thing that does
   something; suffix used to indicate comparing some aspect of two things]

2. **-or** - (one who or that which does something)

   actor, professor, spectator, projector
   [noun suffix; added to a Latin root]

3. **-ar** - (pertaining to)

   solar, singular, globular, polar
   [adjective suffix; used with adjectives other than those that use the
   comparative suffix -er]

4. **-ure** - (state of being)

   pleasure, erasure, pasture, structure
   [noun suffix; often added to a root ending with -s or -t]

(ər.ē´)

1. **-ery** - (combination of suffixes -er and -y)

   finery, cannery, archery, shrubbery
   [noun suffix; added to an Anglo-Saxon root]

2. **-ory** - (combination of suffixes -or and -y)

   factory, directory, accessory, cursory, compulsory
   [noun or adjective suffix; added to a Latin root]

3. **-ary** - (combination of suffixes -ar and -y)

   infirmary, boundary, notary, rotary
   [noun suffix]

(ət)

1. **-et** - (diminutive; often obscure)

   locket, ticket, hatchet, budget
   [noun suffix; added to an Anglo-Saxon root]

2. **-ate** - (pertaining to)

   moderate, delicate, literate, elaborate
   [verb or adjective suffix; when used as an adjective ending the a is
   schwaed]

3. **-ite** - (related to; mineral)

   favorite, opposite, infinite, granite
   [uncommon noun and adjective suffix]

(ē)

1. **-y** - (characterized by; state or quality of; diminutive)

   windy, dusty, willowy, gritty, Billy
   [usually an adjective suffix; usually added to an Anglo-Saxon root]

2. **-ee** - (person)

   employee, refugee, absentee, nominee
   [noun suffix; indicating a person; usually added to a Latin root]

(ē´.ən)

1. **-ian** - (connective -i- with suffix -an; one who)

   guardian, pedestrian, civilian, reptilian
   [variant form of -an used to denote people added to a Latin root]

2. **-ion** - (connective -i- with suffix -on)

   champion, dominion, medallion, rebellion
   [noun suffix; variant form of -on]

(ĭk.əl´)

1. **-ical** - (combination of suffixes -ic and al; of)

   magical, logical, nautical, mythical
   [adjective suffix; variant form of -al; follows the same rules for usage]

2. **-icle** - (variable)

   article, icicle, ventricle, chronicle
   [usually a noun suffix]

(shən)

1. **-tion** - (action or state of)

   motion, action, connection, infection
   [noun suffix; really is connective -i- and suffix -on added to a root
   ending with -t]

2. **-sion** - (action or state of)

   tension, comprehension, discussion, admission
   [noun suffix; really is connective -i- and suffix -on added to a root
   ending with -s or -ss]

3. **-cian** - (person concerned)

   musician, electrician, beautician, dietician
   [noun suffix; combination of -ic, connective -i- and the suffix
   -an; variant form of -an added to a root ending with -ic]

(shəl)

1. **-cial** - (pertaining to)

   facial, racial, official, crucial
   [adjective suffix; combination of -c from the root, connective
   -i-, and suffix -al; variant form of -al added to a root ending with
   -ic]

2. **-tial** - (pertaining to)

   partial, presidential, consequential, confidential
   [adjective suffix; combination of -t from the root, connective -i- and
    suffix -an; variant form of -al added to a root ending with -t]

(shəs)

1. **-cious** - (full of; having)

   spacious, gracious, ferocious, delicious
   [adjective suffix; combination of -c from root, connective -i- and
   suffix -ous; variant form of -ous added to root ending with -c]

2. **-tious** - (full of; having)

   infectious, ambitious, fractious, superstitious
   [adjective suffix; combination of -t from root word, connective
   -i- and suffix -ous; variant form of -ous added to root ending with -t]

V.   Connectives

The vowels i and u are commonly used to connect the root word and a suffix. These patterns are apparently a carry-over from the conjugated form of the word from early Latin or Greek. In some teaching materials, these vowel or vowel/consonant patterns are called "connectives," and because that term seems to describe their function appropriately, it will be used in the following discussion:

Connective u:

1. When the letter u follows the final letter of a root but is not part of the suffix and comes at the end of the syllable, it is pronounced as long u.

    (contin.u. ous, doc.u. ment, vac.u.um)

2. The u may also be found combined with an l. This occurs when the u comes at the end of one syllable and the l combines with the suffix to make the final syllable.

    (pop.u.lous, stim.u.lant, glob.u.lar)

3. When the connecting u follows the letter t (before any suffix), the sound for the t is usually changed to (ch) and the u is sounded as (oo). Thus, tu in this position is usually sounded as (choo).

    (act – actual, tempest – tempestuous, presume – presumptuous)

4. If the connective u or ul follows a root word ending in a d, the sound of the d will change to (j) and the u will sound as ($\overline{oo}$). Thus, du in this position sounds as (j$\overline{oo}$).

    (grad – grad.u.al,   mod – mod.u.lar,   cred – cred.u.lous,   fraud – fraud.u.lent)

Special note: The u of the suffix -ure affects the sound of the final t of a root just as the connective u does. When added to a root word ending in a t, the sound of t will be (ch) and the sound of the suffix will be (er). Together, as -ture, they should be read as (cher). Although -ture is not a true suffix, it is easier for most students to think of t-ure as a unit rather than separate it.

Connective i:

1. The connective letter i is usually pronounced as (ē) and occasionally, after the consonants l and n, as the consonant sound of y.

    | rad.i.ate | med.i.um | obliv.i.ous | accord.i.on |
    | cur.i.ous | rebell.i.on | mill.i.on | delir.i.ous |
    | civil.i.an | super.i.or | un.i.on | |

Dictionaries vary in their printed indication for this sound. The student should be taught to first try the pronunciation as long ē. If the word pronounced does not sound familiar, it should then be sounded using the i as the consonant sound of y.

If the student is able to read words that result from adding suffixes to root words ending in y, (happiest; silliness) he/she will have little difficulty learning to read and spell words using the connective i. In this rule, the student learns that the final y changed to an i maintains the sound of long e or long i, whichever it represented in the original root word.

    lady – ladies, funny – funnier, testimony – testimonial, imply – implied

Since the changed final y most often sounds as long e, the student should learn that sound as the first one for the connective i. If it does not provide a word which she/he recognizes, then the long i sound should be tried. When the student still does not recognize the word, the dictionary should be consulted.

2. When the connective i follows a root word that ends in the letter g, the i signals the soft sound for the g (j), and the i is silent.

    legion, region, religious, contagious, egregious

3. When the connective i follows a root word ending in c, t, s, or x, it signals a change of pronunciation for those letters, usually to (sh), and the -i- is usually silent.

    face – facial, politic – politician, grace – gracious,

    instruct – instruction, infect – infections, part – partial,

    tense – tension, compress – compression,

    suffice – sufficient, obnoxious

Occasionally, the connective i changes the sound of the letters t and c to (sh) and is also pronounced as long e.

    negotiate, associate

The student must be taught to realize the difference in the sound of the letter c (sh) when it is followed by a connective i and the final c(s) when it is followed by a suffix beginning with an i.

    face – facing – but facial, grace – gracing – but gracious,

    specify – special, electric – electricity — but electrician, publicize, mysticism, lucid

I.   Introduction to Roots

fix	port	tract	mit	script	ceed	cycl
			miss	scribe	cede, cess	

The English language has evolved using innumerable root forms that come primarily from the Anglo-Saxon, Latin, and Greek languages. These roots combine with different prefixes and suffixes to make many thousands of words used in everyday language, as well as words used in more advanced and technical language. Most of the words with Latin and Greek roots follow phonetic patterns. In most of these roots, the vowel pronunciations are regularly phonetic, but some will change with the addition of affixes. Some roots have more than one form or spelling (mit/miss, pel/puls, cede/ceed/sede/cess), and a student ready for language structure at this level should be introduced to two or three possibilities at the same time. The order of presentation of the roots can be even more varied than that of the affixes. Obviously, some roots occur more often and combine more frequently with affixes to make commonly used words. Logic dictates that the more commonly used roots with simple meanings should be introduced first, one or two at a time. Others can be added when those are mastered. A suggested order is provided below, but it can be used with flexibility. The student can be given the opportunity to choose which ones to learn next.

The information printed on the back of the root cards includes very simple meanings and examples of words using the root. At the bottom of some of the cards is a row of words showing the variations the root might take; examples of an unusual form found in a common word are noted in italics.

Order of Presentation of Roots

This is a suggested order of teaching the roots. It is not "carved in stone." The teacher should consider the student's interests and school subjects when presenting this list. The asterisks (***) at the bottom of the third list indicate that there are other roots to be considered later.

port	scrib/script	lect/leg/lig
tract	spect/spec/spic	mot/mob/mov
rupt	struct	nat
fer	tend/tens/tent	put
fus	vent/ven	sist
ject	voc/vok	stant/stanc
vert/vers	ced/ceed/cess	stitu
pel/puls	fix	strict/string/strain
ply/plic	claim/clam	test
tain/ten/tent/tin	duct/duc	numer
clud/clus	fect/fic/fict	capt/capit
cur	fin	cid/cis
dic/dict	act	gest
flect/flex	quir/quis/quest	junct/join/joint
form	sent/sens	jur/jud/just
gress/grad	spir	ord/ordin
mit/miss	vis/vid	pass
pend/pens	caus/cus	rect/reg
pos/posit	cept/ceiv/ceit	sum/sumpt
		***

II.   Supplementary List of Roots

The roots presented on the cards are the common ones, with which the students should begin their studies. For instructors working with advanced students and adults, the supplementary list below provides additional roots. For teachers and students wishing to study root forms and derivations in greater depth, a good resource is Amsel Greene's book, *Word Clues, the Vocabulary Builder,* published by Glencoe Publishing Company; Blacklick, Ohio.

As with the roots listed on the cards, some spelling variations, noted in parentheses, can be found in this list.

1.   astro (star): astrophysics, astrology, astronaut (asterisk, disaster)

2.   chrom (color): chrome, polychrome

3.   chron (time): chronic, synchronize

4.   cogn, gno (know): cognition, recognize, diagnosis

5.   corp, corps (body): corpse, incorporate, corpulent

6.   cycl (circle, wheel): cyclone, bicycle, encyclical

7.   lat (carry, bring): relate, legislator, superlative

8.   liter (letter): literal, illiterate, obliterate

9.   locut, loqu (speak): interlocutory, elocution, loquacious, soliloquy

10. log (word, reason): logic, logistics, logopedics

11. luc, lumin (light): lucid, elucidate, illumination, luminescence

12. mania, (mad; obsession with): maniac, pyromania, kleptomania, maniacal

13. matr, mater (mother): matrimony, matriarch, maternity

14. mor, mort (death): morbid, immortality, mortician

15. morph (form): morpheme, morphology, endomorph

16. nov (new): novel, innovate

17. path (feeling): pathological, pathetic, sympathy, pathos

18. patr, pater (father): patricide, patron, paternal

19. pet (ask, attach): petition, compete, impetuous (repeat)

20. phob (fear): hydrophobia, claustrophobia

21. plet, ple (fill): complete, supplement

22. pon, pound (place): component, impound

23. pot, poss (power): potent, impossible, possessive

24. prim (first): prime, primogenitor, primitive

25. scend, scent, scens (climb): ascend, descent, condescension

26. sci (know): science, unconscious, conscientious

27. secut, sequ (follow): persecute, consecutive, sequence, sequential

28. sid, sed (sit): preside, resident, dissident, sedentary

29. simil, simul, semble (like, together): similar, simultaneous, resemblance

30. soci (unite): society, sociology, social, associate

31. stat (stand): static, reinstate, statistic, statue

32. tact, tang (touch): tactile, contact, intangible, tangent

33. techn (skill, art): technical, technique, technology

34. tempo (time): tempo, temporary, contemporaneous

35. therm (heat): thermos, thermometer, diathermy

36. tut, tui (guard, teach): tutor, tuition, intuitive

37. vac (empty): evacuate, vacant

38. vi (away): deviate, impervious, via, viaduct

39. volv, volu (roll): revolve, convolution, voluminous

15.   TEACHING GRAMMAR

The requirement to teach English grammar to students, as well as the methodology employed, is controversial. This debate also exists among teachers who work with students with language learning disabilities. Just as dyslexia makes the acquisition of decoding and encoding skills difficult for students, it also seems to affect their ability to master grammatical concepts and identify the names and uses of the various parts of speech. The dyslexic student needs not only direct and sequential instruction in sound/syllable relationships, syllable division rules and patterns, but also direct and sequential instruction in mastering parts of speech. Knowing and using information about grammar helps clarify the writings of others; it also helps students achieve greater clarity in their own writing style.

Some educators argue that teaching grammar in such detail and depth makes the process of writing too mechanical, therefore impeding creativity. Those who maintain this argument must understand that there are students for whom the "creativity" or "flow" will not be released until the mechanics of the basic process are understood and have been practiced enough for them to become automatic. Then the cognitive strengths of dyslexic students will be reflected in their written work.

The basic philosophy for teaching a language disabled student also applies to teaching grammar. Introduce one grammatical concept, a part of speech, and provide the practice necessary for mastery. Teach and practice another concept and then show the student how the two relate. Repeat this process until all the grammatical elements are taught.

Linguistically, it seems logical to begin with nouns. The concept of nouns and their use should be discussed and practiced until the student has a clear understanding of that part of speech and can recognize nouns in the writing of others and in his/her own writing. The teacher then moves on to another part of speech, perhaps adjectives to describe the nouns or verbs to describe the action of the nouns. After each new part of speech is introduced and practiced, the student must be taught how it fits with the other parts of speech already learned. Following these steps also provides the consistent review needed by these students.

The mastery of labels for the various parts of speech, in and of itself, is of no value for any student. Only when the student has the basic understanding of the <u>function</u> of each grammatical category can that information be used to enhance reading and writing skills. The use of this information can be thought of in two ways:

1. When reading, a dyslexic student who has auditory processing difficulties needs to trim the "excess verbiage" from longer, more complex written passages. For these students, too many words becomes "verbal clutter" and makes it difficult to determine the basic point the author is making. In order to improve comprehension, the student first needs to recognize primary nouns and verbs and eliminate the adjectives and adverbs, which the author has used to make the writing more interesting.

2. In order to produce acceptable written work, dyslexic students must get their thoughts down in a logical sequence, using simple words which they feel confident spelling. Once the sequence and organization of the primary ideas are satisfactory, the student can then go back and enhance what has been written. He/she can find the nouns used and add adjectives to enhance them. The same can be done for verbs, using adverbs. When the skeleton of an idea is exposed, it can be fleshed out with many intriguing words.

If students know the classifications of adjectives (personality, ownership, physical characteristics, number, defining phrases), they can consider each one and use terms from their vocabulary to supply them. Knowing the use of adverbs and the categories within that classification (how, when, where, why, how much), students can consider each of these and again use appropriate vocabulary to amplify their writing. A thesaurus is a valuable source for higher level vocabulary words that are known but sometimes not easily recalled. Understanding adverbs and how they are used allows a student to consider their placement or relocation in the sentence to make compositions more interesting.

Since abstract verbal concepts and labels are sometimes difficult for the dyslexic student to grasp, the introduction of some concrete memory aids for learning the various parts of speech is extremely helpful, and essential for some. Educators have used a variety of aids with fairly consistent and positive results. The old fashioned system of diagraming sentences with horizontal and slanted lines to denote various components introduces a pictorial memory factor to support the weaker verbal memory. For teachers who have forgotten or were never taught diagraming sentences, a brief review can be found in the Appendix on page 71. We can also recommend some of the older English textbooks: *Handbook of English* (a set of standard English texts which can be used to help with diagraming) by John E. Warinner, published by Harcourt, Brace; *Exercises in English Grammar, Books I and II* (a simplified but well organized and clearly written resource), by John H. Treanor, published by EPS; *A Skeleton In Every Closet* developed by Project Read in the Bloomington, Minnesota, Public Schools, though it uses a different symbol for the various parts of speech, is a helpful resource. Their address is:

Project Read
Project Read/Language Circle
Language Circle Enterprises
P.O. Box 20631
Bloomington, MN 55402

16. ROTE MEMORY WORDS

Lists of elementary words to be memorized can be found in the *Language Tool Kit*. The words listed below are more advanced and are required for students studying the English language at this level. These words, some phonetic for reading but with irregular spelling patterns, and others irregular for both, need to be rote memorized. In general, they have been arranged according to the degree of difficulty and the frequency of occurrence. The teacher should introduce the words starting down the left hand column and then progressing through the other columns, proceeding in the same manner with the columns on the following page. The list extends to quite an advanced vocabulary level. Each student should be expected to master only those words which are appropriate for his or her vocabulary level.

Some students will be able to read many of these words. The known words should be reviewed occasionally, with a few new ones added from time to time, until the entire list is mastered. The student should know the meanings of the words and be able to use them in sentences.

The majority of dyslexic students will not know how to spell most of these words correctly. The teacher should find out which ones the student can already spell. Then a few of the remaining words should be assigned for memorizing, perhaps no more than five at a time. The number can be adjusted to each student's needs and ability to memorize. The student will learn the words more easily if the letter names are said aloud as the letters are being written, since this provides simultaneous auditory, kinesthetic, and visual reinforcement. For words which cause particular problems, the student and/or the teacher can use mnemonics to help memorization: phrases such as "hoarding coarse boards" or "paper stationery," or over-pronouncing words such as parliament, subtle, or solder. The older student can be assigned words to study independently; however, the teacher must review these words until they have been mastered for spelling.

ache	muscle	receipt	awful
acre	scissors	canoe	charity
breathe	schedule	err	clarify
truly	purpose	fortune	era
wholly	scarce	experiment	fiery
police	knowledge	separate	query
character	southern	handsome	parallel
choir	bury	medicine	depot
angel	board	lawyer	vacuum
inn	hoard	sandwich	guarantee
mitt	hoarse	vegetable	menu
watt	coarse	lettuce	mischief
ebb	course	raspberries	soldier
gross	court	cupboard	frontier
kilo	promise	purchase	dessert
etc.	piano	bald	desert
garage	treble	scald	plateau
tongue	recipe	awe	canvas
species	tariff	subtle	lacquer
comrade	brochure	debris	miniature

league	parliament	prestige	boulevard
margarine	bureau	regime	lava
restaurant	portrait	shepherd	ballet
anxious	possess	palace	fillet
anxiety	control	furnace	gourmet
luxury	patrol	menace	bouquet
cemetery	exhaust	grimace	hearth
issue	exhibit	solace	salmon
tissue	luncheon	surface	forfeit
cushion	dungeon	personnel	heifer
fashion	surgeon	lieu	reservoir
plaid	pigeon	simile	khaki
conquest	hygiene	mediocre	tarpaulin
heir	morale	massacre	memoir
herb	mortgage	fiancé	licorice
hurrah	nausea	fiancée	silhouette
giraffe	amateur	matinée	naive
gauge	chauffeur	finale	cordial
sword	aisle	diamond	rendezvous
suspicion	biscuit	diaper	rapport
lye	idol	mosquito	repertoire
rye	exempt	sovereign	impromptu
dye	unkempt	colonel	ukulele
dyeing	handkerchief	lieutenant	limousine
dying	sieve	sergeant	leopard
lying	waive	corps	jeopardy
questionnaire	stationery	numerical	ewe
millionaire	indict	herald	isle
resumé	yacht	extol	isthmus
alm	wharf	solder	sapphire
palm	tomb	facade	elite
calm	womb	bough	espionage
qualm	sulphur	suite	impasse
psalm	epic	beige	lingerie
liquor	epoch	trough	harangue

17. AFTERTHOUGHTS

➤ If you teach a student to spell in English, he/she will be able to read. If you teach a student to read English, that does not ensure that he/she will be able to spell.

➤ A teacher with knowledge of English language structure and appropriate teaching techniques can be flexible within the boundaries of the system, while adhering to the essential teaching principles.

➤ Teachers cannot successfully teach what they do not know and understand.

➤ Recent strides in brain and pedagogical research have contributed to the understanding and increased interest in the Orton Gillingham approach.

➤ Remember that you are working with students who have struggled to learn to read and spell; they have scars.

➤ The English language is interesting, challenging, and complicated, with roots from many other languages. In reading and spelling, the patterns of letters are more predictable in other languages. However, it is reassuring to remember, according to computer analysis, the English language is 86% predictable if one knows phonics and spelling rules and patterns. The higher level of language structure is, in many ways, more predictable than that found at the elementary level. The teacher will gradually need to master the intricacies of the language in order to pass them on to a student. The student will need to be encouraged to realize that this type of drillwork is essential for mastering the language. It becomes a fascinating lifetime study.

➤ If a student or a parent objects to the idea of repetitive drill, the teacher can share Dr. Sylvia Richardson's thoughts on the topic. Dr. Richardson is a Distinguished Professor of Communication Sciences and Clinical Professor of Pediatrics, at the University of South Florida, in Tampa. At a national conference of the International Dyslexia Association, she referred to the fact that Olympic athletes practice one skill or even one small component of a skill repeatedly, for weeks or months, and are not criticized or made fun of; in fact such practice is expected for championship performance. She questioned why then should teachers avoid or apologize for asking a student who is having difficulty with written language to practice repeatedly the skills necessary to master something as important as learning to read and spell words, learning comprehension skills, or writing thoughts clearly and accurately?

I. Check Lists

A. Basic Language Sounds

The following is a list of the sound units, rules, and syllable patterns included in the *Language Tool Kit*. When the teacher checks those known to the student, she/he will then have a record of those units that still need to be taught.

Short Vowels:
a__
e__ ea__
i__ y__
o__
u__ a__ o__ ou__

Long Vowels:
a__ a-e__ ai__ ay__ eigh__ ei__ ey__
e__ ee__ ea__ y__ e-e__ ie__ ei__ ey__
i__ i-e__ igh__ y__ ie__ y-e__
o__ o-e__ oa__ ow__ ou__ oe__
u__ u-e__ ue__ eu__ ew__

Other Vowel Patterns:
au__ aw__ o__ augh__ ough__
oi__ oy__
oo__ ew__ u__ u-e__ ou__ ue__ ui__ eu__
oo__ u__
ou__ ow__

r-Controlled:
ar__
ear__
er__ ir__ ur__ or__ ar__ ear__ yr__
or__

Consonants:
b__
c__ k__ -ck__ ch__ -que__
d__ -ed__
f__ ph__ gh__

Consonants: (cont.)
g__ gh__ -gue__
h__
j__ g__ -dge__
l__
m__ -mb__ -mn__
n__ kn__ gn__
p__
qu__
r__ wr__ rh__
s__ c__ sc__
t__ -ed__
v__
w__
x__
y__
z__ s__

Consonant Digraphs:
ch__ -tch__
sh__ ch__
th__ th__
wh__

Consonant Syllables:
ble__ cle__ ckle__ dle__ fle__
gle__ ple__ tle__ zle__
stle__

Common Suffixes:
-ed__
-ly__
-tion__
-sion__

Ending Combinations:

-ing__ -ang__ -ong__ -ung__ -eng__

-ink__ -ank__ -onk__ -unk__

Irregular Combinations:

-alk__ alt__

all__

-ind__

-ild__

old__

-ost__

qua__

wa__

war__

wor__

Adding Suffix Rules:

Just adding__

Adding to roots with
short vowel__

Adding to roots ending
with -e__

Adding to roots ending
with -y__

Syllable Patterns

(C) Closed__

(L) Consonant-le__

(O) Open__

(V) Vowel teams__

(E) Vowel Consonant -e__

(R) r controlled__

Syllable Division Rules:

VC.CV__

V.CV__

VC.V__

consonant-le__

word.word__

V.V__

B.   Prefixes

The following is a list of the more common word units included in the prefix deck of this kit. Each unit has one or two lines after it, one for each of the sounds a student needs to learn for that unit. It is helpful to know that the single vowel in a prefix has one of three possibilities—it may be long, short, or schwaed. The single vowel in an open syllable prefix may be long, short or schwaed; the vowel in a closed syllable prefix may be short or schwaed.

a- ___ ___   im- ___
ab- ___ ___   inter- ___
ac- ___ ___   ir- ___
ad- ___ ___   mal- ___ ___
af- ___ ___   mid- ___
ag- ___ ___   mis- ___
al- ___ ___ ___   non- ___
an- ___ ___   ob- ___ ___
ap- ___ ___   oc- ___ ___
ar- ___ ___   of- ___ ___
as- ___ ___   op- ___ ___
at- ___ ___   out- ___
be- ___   over- ___
bi- ___   per- ___
co- ___   post- ___ ___
col- ___ ___   pre- ___ ___
com- ___ ___   pro- ___ ___
con- ___ ___   re- ___ ___
cor- ___ ___   se- ___
de- ___ ___   sub- ___
di- ___ ___   suc- ___
dif- ___   suf- ___
dis- ___   sum- ___
e- ___ ___   sup- ___
ef- ___ ___   super- ___
em- ___ ___   sur- ___
en- ___   sus- ___
ex- ___ ___   trans- ___
for- ___   tri- ___
fore- ___   un- ___ ___
in- ___   uni- ___
il- ___   with- ___

B.   Prefixes (continued)

The following is a list of the more advanced prefixes.

ante- ___

anti- ___ ___

auto- ___ ___

circum- ___ ___

contra- ___

counter- ___

dia- ___ ___

dys- ___

epi- ___ ___

equi- ___ ___

geo- ___ ___

homo- ___ ___

hyper- ___

hypo- ___ ___

intra- ___

intro- ___

micro- ___ ___

mono- ___ ___

multi- ___

pan- ___

para- ___

photo- ___ ___

poly- ___ ___

psycho- ___ ___

semi- ___

syl- ___

sym- ___

syn- ___

tele- ___ ___

C.   Suffixes

The following is a list of the more common word units included in the suffix deck of this kit. Each unit has one, two, or three lines after it, one for each of the sounds a student needs to learn for that unit. It is helpful to know that the single letter vowel in a suffix usually has only one of two possibilities—it may be short or schwaed. Because they come at the end of a word and often are not the accented syllable, many of the suffixes have schwaed vowel sounds.

-able ___	-ical ___
-ade ___	-id ___
-age ___	-ify ___
-ain ___	-ile ___ ___
-al ___	-ing ___
-an ___	-ish ___
-ance ___	-ist ___
-ant ___	-ition ___
-ar ___	-ity ___
-ard ___	-ive ___
-ary ___ ___	-ize ___
-ate ___ ___	-less ___
-ation ___	-ling ___
-dom ___	-ly ___
-ed ___ ___ ___	-ment ___
-ee ___	-most ___
-el ___	-ness ___
-en ___	-on ___ ___
-ence ___	-or ___
-ent ___	-ous ___
-er ___	-s ___ ___
-ery ___	-ship ___
-es ___	-sion ___ ___
-ess ___	-some ___
-est ___	-ster ___
-et ___	-th ___
-fold ___	-tion ___
-ful ___	-tude ___
-fy ___	-ture ___
-hood ___	-ty ___
-ible ___	-ward ___
-ic ___	-y ___

C. Suffixes (continued)

The following is a list of the more advanced suffixes.

-ability ___   -ious___
-ality ___   -ism___
-arity ___   -ite ___ ___
-cial ___   -itis ___
-cian ___   -ium ___
-cious ___   -lent ___
-cle ___   -logue ___
-crat, cracy ___ ___ -lent ___
-cy ___   -mony ___
-eer ___   -oid ___
-esce ___   -ology ___
-escence ___   -onym ___
-escent ___   -orous ___
-ese ___   -ory ___ ___
-ette ___   -osis ___
-ial ___   -osity ___
-ian ___   -ry ___
-ibility ___   -sis ___
-ically ___   -tial ___
-ice ___   -tious ___
-ile ___   -ule ___
-ine ___ ___ ___   -ure ___
-ion___   -us ___
-ior___

D. Roots

The following is a list of the more common word units included in this kit. Each unit has one, two, or three lines after it, one for each of the sounds a student needs to learn for that unit. It is helpful to know that the single vowel in a closed syllable root has only one of two possibilities—it may be short or schwaed; in a two syllable root, the vowel sounds may vary, depending upon the syllable division and the accent placement on the root when an affix is added.

act ___

capt, capit ___ ___

caus, cus ___ ___

ced, ceed, cess ___ ___ ___

cept, ceiv, ceit ___ ___ ___

cid, cis ___ ___

claim, clam ___ ___

clud, clus ___ ___

cur ___

dic, dict ___ ___

duc, duct ___ ___

fect, fic, fict ___ ___ ___

fer ___

fin, finit ___ ___

fix ___

flect, flex ___ ___

form ___

fus ___

gest ___

gress, grad ___ ___

ject ___

junct, join, joint ___ ___ ___

jur, jud, just ___ ___ ___

lect, leg, lig ___ ___ ___

mit, miss ___ ___

nat ___

numer ___

ord, ordin ___ ___

pass ___

pel, puls ___ ___

pend, pens ___ ___

ply, plic ___ ___

port ___

pos, posit ___ ___

put ___

quir, quis, quest ___ ___ ___

rect, reg ___ ___

rupt ___

scrib, script ___ ___

sent, sens ___ ___

sist ___

spect, spec, spic ___ ___ ___

spir ___

stant, stanc ___ ___

stitu ___

strict, string, strain ___ ___ ___

struct ___

sum, sumpt ___ ___

tain, ten, tent, tin ___ ___ ___ ___

tend, tens, tent ___ ___ ___

test ___

tract ___

trud, trus ___ ___

vent, ven ___ ___

vert, vers ___ ___

vis, vid ___ ___

voc vok ___ ___

The following is a list of the more advanced roots.

annu, enni ___ ___	mand, mend ___
arch ___	med ___
aud ___	mem ___
centr ___	merg, mers ___ ___
cit ___	meter, metr ___ ___
cord, cour ___ ___	min ___
cred ___	mod ___
fac, fact ___ ___	mut ___
flict ___	nom ___
flu ___	par ___
fort, forc ___ ___	ped, pod ___ ___
gen ___	phon ___
graph, gram ___ ___	scop ___
greg ___	solv, solut ___ ___
leg ___	son ___
loc ___	spher ___
lud, lus ___ ___	tort ___
	trib ___
	val, vail ___ ___
	vict, vinc ___ ___
	viv, vita ___ ___

II.   Accent Placement Rules

It is important to note that the rules governing accent placement are variable. For students who experience problems learning to read and spell, learning the concepts and patterns involved is valuable. With a good deal of practice, applying accents and determining schwa will become almost automatic for most students.

1. There is almost always an accent on the first or second syllable of a word with three or more syllables, also there is usually a second accent as well.

    com.′bin.a.′tion   dis.′ap.pear′ance

2. Tips for accenting first syllables in two syllable words:

    (a)   Two like consonants following the first vowel– (shop′ping, pen′nant)
    (b)   -ck syllables with words ending in -et– (pock′et, jack′et)
    (c)   consonant -le syllables are never accented– (han′dle, rid′dle)

3. Tips for accenting the final syllable in two syllable words:

    (a)   The accent is most often on the root word and not the prefix– (re.tain′, in.vade′, pro.mote′).
    (b)   If the single vowel in the last of a two syllable word is clearly short, the accent is on that syllable– (com.pel′, for.bid′, pre.dict′).
          (**Note**: the final r in confer and occur is doubled to denote the accent placement (confer′red and occur′ring) to keep the vowel from having its long sound (ēr) as in (interfere) or (ūr) as in (curing).
    (c)   If the root word, with a suffix added, has two similar consonants before the suffix, the accent is on the syllable just before the double consonant– (be′.gin – be.gin′.ning, com.mit′ – com.mit′.tee, for.got′ – for.got.′ten).

4. Other Patterns:

    (a)   In words of more than two syllables ending in silent -e, count back and accent the third syllable from the end– (com′plic.ate, def′in.ite, mod′.ern.ize).
    (b)   Parts of speech   noun – (reb.′el)   verb – (re.bel′)
          affects accent: noun – (con.′duct)   verb – (con.duct′)

5. Suffixes:

    (a)   The accent always falls on the syllable preceding:
          -it.y   real – re.al′ity, human – hu.man′ity, pop′ular – pop.u.lar′ity
          -ic   gi.gan′tic, e.las′tic
          -ic.al   his.tor′ic.al, po.lit′ic.al
    (b)   The accent on the suffix:
          -oon   har.poon′, la.goon′
          -eer   en.gin.eer′, auc.tion.eer′
          -ment   followed by another suffix: in′stru.ment – in.stru.ment′al, el′e.ment – el.e.ment′ary, ar′gu.ment – ar.gu.ment′a.tive

6. Connectives:

    (a)   (-i, -u, -ul, -ol)– the accent usually falls on the vowel directly ahead of them– (ra′diate, stren′uous, vocab′ulary, red′olent, interme′diary, ambig′uous).

    (b)   (-ti, -si, -xi)– the accent is always on the vowel which precedes (sh) sound (except in words ending in -ity) (sta′tion, combina′tion, impress′ion, apprehen′sion, gra′cious, an′xious, im.par′.tial.ity).

7. Other suffixes and endings:

-cracy	democ′racy, theoc′racy
-ology	biol′ogy, mythol′ogy
-meter	thermom′eter, altim′eter
-graphy	biog′raphy, teleg′raphy
-pathy	antip′athy, telep′athy
-itis	tonsili′tis, bronchi′tis

III.   Lesson Plan

Name: _____ **Date:** _____ **Lesson #** _____

Review:

    Old Material:

    New Material:

Visual drill:

Basic sounds: Prefixes: Suffixes: Roots:

Auditory drill:

Basic sounds: Prefixes: Suffixes: Roots:

Blending drill:

Sounds: Words:

Introduction of new material:

Spelling:

Reading:

    Material:

    Beginning page #:

Non-phonetic words:

Homework Assignment:

Summary:

1.

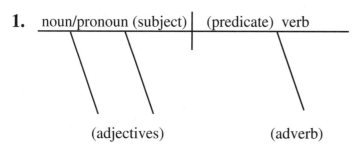

Example: The fat puppy played happily.

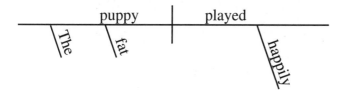

2.

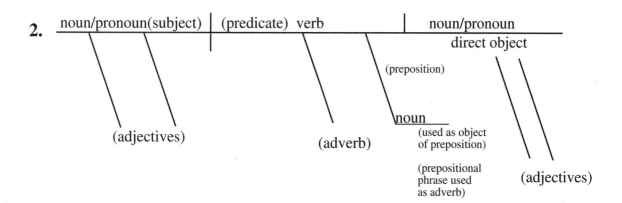

Example: The college student quickly studied his chemistry textbook in the library.

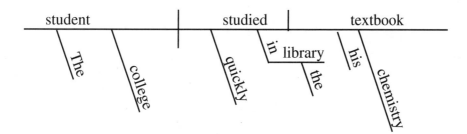

3.

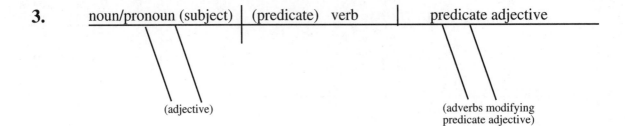

Example: Three pretty girls were very early yesterday.

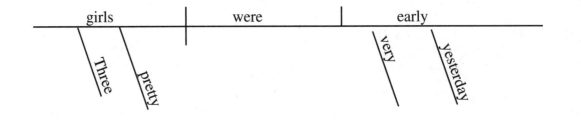

4.

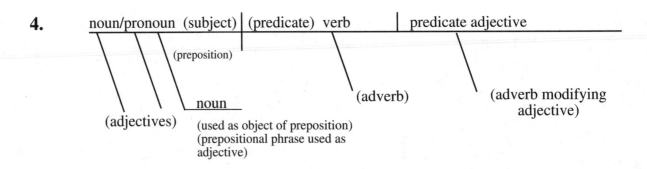

Example: The mountain bike against the oak tree was extremely expensive.

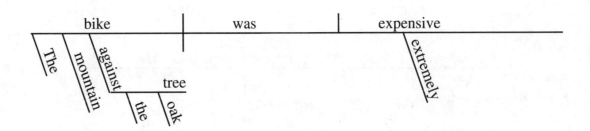

72

5.

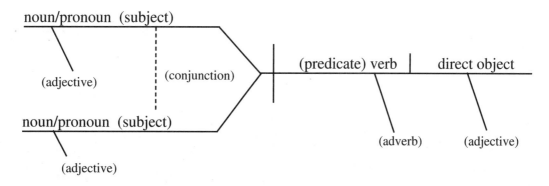

Example: One boy and two girls gladly helped their grandmother.

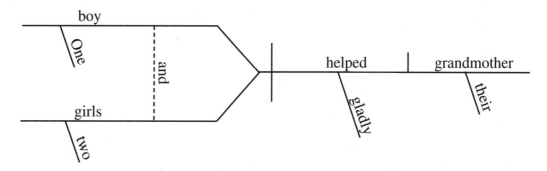

6.

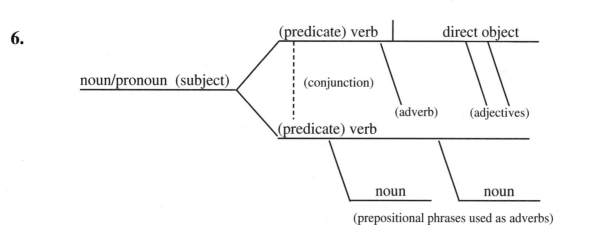

(prepositional phrases used as adverbs)

Example: He quickly climbed the tall tree and rested for a while in the tree house.

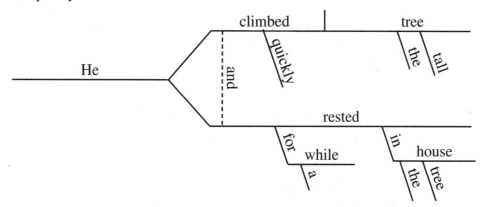

7.

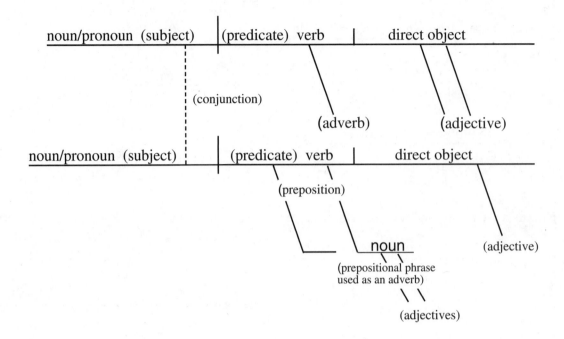

noun/pronoun (subject) | (predicate) verb | direct object

(conjunction)

(adverb) (adjective)

noun/pronoun (subject) | (predicate) verb | direct object

(preposition)

noun

(prepositional phrase used as an adverb)

(adjectives)

(adjective)

Example: Because he could not reach the top shelf, Bobby asked his father for help with the heavy box.

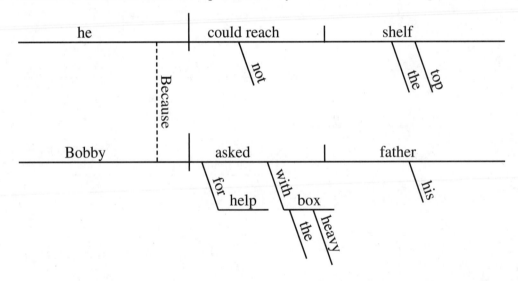